The Tapestry of Caring

INTERPRETIVE PERSPECTIVES ON EDUCATION AND POLICY

George W. Noblit and William T. Pink, Series Editors

The Tapestry of Caring: Education as Nurturance

Edited by

A. Renee Prillaman
The Hearth Foundation Institute
The University of North Carolina at Chapel Hill

Deborah J. Eaker
North Carolina State University

Doris M. Kendrick
Appalachian State University

ABLEX PUBLISHING CORPORATON
NORWOOD, NEW JERSEY

Printed in the United States of America

Library of Congress Cataloging-in-Publication Data

The Tapestry of caring : education as nurturance / edited by A. Renee
    Prillaman, Deborah J. Eaker, Doris M. Kendrick.
        p.   cm. — (Interpretive perspectives on education and policy)
    Includes bibliographical references and index.
    ISBN 0-89391-971-3. — ISBN 1-56750-075-7 (pbk.)
    1. Moral education. 2. Caring. I. Prillaman, A. Renee.
II. Eaker, Deborah J. II. Kendrick, Doris M. IV. Series.
LC268.T28   1994
370.11′4—dc20   93-46343
                                                                  CIP

Ablex Publishing Company
355 Chestnut Street
Norwood, New Jersey 07648

We dedicate this book to our children
Caitlin, Andrew, Erika, Amanda, Melissa,
and the little one soon to be born
with the commitment that their education
nurtures them to be fully who they are.

Contents

Acknowledgments

This book largely grew out of a group that was created by George Noblit and Jim Paul. Their idea to gather with interested colleagues to discuss the nature of caring in education was the first thread in the tapestry of this book. We are grateful to them and to the members of the group. George continued to provide guidance, support, and encouragement throughout the project.

The book was ultimately made possible by the chapter authors. Their commitment to an ethic of caring in education will always be treasured by us. We indeed also appreciate their timely submission of chapters and responsiveness to suggestions.

We would like to express our gratitude to Joanne Palmer at Ablex. She saw the book through to its actual birth at the most critical period. She was patient, persistent, and supportive.

Finally, we wish to thank our husbands, Hugh, Rob, and Bryant, and our parents. They have taught us the meaning of being cared for.

Introduction

The Weave And The Weaver: A Tapestry Begun

A. Renee Prillaman
Deborah J. Eaker

This book is intended to ground the theories of caring in education and, in doing so, expand the current discourse on caring. Grounding in education is possible because of the work of those who have theorized and studied caring, such as Belenky, Clinchy, Goldberger, and Tarule (1986), Gilligan (1982; Gilligan, Ward, & Taylor, 1988; Gilligan Lyons, & Haumer 1990), and Noddings (1984). The work of these authors is represented in each chapter of this volume. It is appropriate, then, for us to introduce this book with a brief review of their arguments. We will use their work as a basis for expanding the discourse about the ethic of caring in a pragmatic and functional way.

The work of those who have examined the ethic of caring has provided a rich and useful discussion of the topic from people who, no doubt, are caring and are committed to caring in practice. However, we have found sorely missing the presentation of real-life expressions of caring educational contexts. In this book we address what is missing by providing a collection of current expressions of educators' and researchers' experiences as they seek to manifest caring.

It is not our intention to subsume the caring discourse further under the domain of academia. Our belief is that the current conception of caring is limited by the very language and structure of academics. To expand this conception, we argue that a

1

shift is required. Thus, we intend to shift the consideration of caring from the domain of academics into the domain where it actually exists—within the self-expression of individuals and in their view of their work, in this case, within educational settings. This is not to say that the current academic works are not important to consider—they are a place to start. We posit that the discourse can be expanded. To do so, we must have an opening created where one does not presently exist.

We intend to create such an opening by taking the discourse from one of theorizing to one that includes the actual work and voices of practitioners within education. Duckworth (1985) described a conspicuous absence of the thoughts and beliefs of practitioners, both in the research literature and in policy making, as akin to holding a national debate on dental health in which the views of dentists are ignored. To begin to fill this gap, this book is intended to more fully include the much needed voices of practitioners in education. We also intend to address caring in education from the perspectives of both women and men. While much of the caring literature suggests that caring is not a quality solely possessed by women, forms of caring that may have more traditionally belonged to men are generally excluded. We see much about how caring "should be" within schools and classrooms, but rarely how it is for the women, men, and children who are already living their lives in caring communities. While it could be argued that the quality of caring could be improved, or that those living in educational communities could better articulate their practices of caring, little can be moved forward without the recognition of a variety of expressions of caring. What we assert is that there is an innate human drive to care.

In order to address what impedes an opening in the current discourse as a possibility, we must first look at the recognized cultural perspective of caring, at what people have said and written about caring. We will do this through examining existing literature in this chapter. Second, through the cases presented in this book, we will expand the literature on caring through the examination of current educational practice. This examination will enable us to see who decides what caring is, particularly in the educational domains of schools, educators, children, and the larger community. Close examination and analysis of practice allows us to look at the concept of caring and what actually drives it in practice. Such an examination should enable a shift in changing the direction of what and who, appropriately, should drive the discourse about caring education. We suggest that what is written in the current literature, at least in the field of education, is theory rather than practice driven and thus may not be fully useful to the professionals who work in educational settings. The cases presented here are seen as individual strands or threads that, woven together, present a tapestry representative of caring in the educational community. A tapestry of caring will reveal the webs of relationships that overlap in various educational settings. It will enable us to explore the personal interconnections with which the everyday lives of the practitioners and students of schooling are woven. Toward the end of creating a rich, full tapestry, each case presented here reflects the multiple colors and textures of the individual author's and informant's self-expressions of caring.

TWO DIVERGENT STRANDS OF DISCOURSE

Educational practitioners often talk about the art and the science of their profession and work. A practitioner, like a weaver, experiences his or her work in at least two aspects: that of being technically correct at one's work, and that of reflecting the deepest self in relationship to that work and communicating it to others. It is these two aspects—the technical and the expressive—that are represented by two strands of discourse on education in academe. These two strands continue to affect educational practice and give conflicting messages to both practitioners and the public. In order to ground our discussion of caring in educational experiences, we have chosen to examine the theoretical discourse on caring, an expressive language, as well as the views of researchers regarding effective teaching, the language of the technical. These two academic strands of discourse have occurred simultaneously but are rather conflicting approaches to education that produce divergent results. To begin this overview, we will first outline the major views of research on effective teaching.

The Discourse on Effective Teaching: The Language of the Technical

The research on teaching has shifted over time as the views of researchers regarding effective teaching have shifted. Medley (1979) describes these shifts in the following way:

> At first effectiveness was perceived as the result of certain personality traits and research was geared to identifying those traits. Later, effectiveness was seen not so much as a function of the characteristics of the teacher, but of the methods of teaching used, and research focused on methods of teaching. Then effectiveness was seen as mainly dependent on the climate the teacher created and maintained in the classroom. More recently, effectiveness has been viewed as a mastery of a repertoire of competencies, and finally there has been increasing emphasis on the ability to display these competencies appropriately, that is, on professional decision making. (p.12)

Since the early 1970s and Rosenshine's (1971) work with teacher effectiveness, a massive body of research has emerged identifying and verifying behaviors consistently observable in effective teachers. The effective teacher is defined in the literature as one who can perform the behaviors that contribute to high student achievement as measured by standardized achievement tests. The behaviors range from maintaining high time on task (Bloom, 1974) to making rules and guidelines clear to students (Brooks, 1985).

Checklists and rating scales have been created by a number of researchers to evaluate the demonstration of competencies. As a result, teacher-training institutes have been encouraged to focus their programs on helping students develop these competencies. The core of what is being advocated is best stated by Medley (1979):

> It is what a teacher does rather than what a teacher is that matters. What a student in a preservice teacher education program needs is to learn not what he should be but what he must do in order to be effective. (p. 13)

This discourse, what we have called the *language of the technical*, was certainly needed 20 years ago, when it originated. It continues to inform us about what certain appropriate practices might be for an educator to be considered technically effective as a teacher. However, just as the weaver would never be satisfied with merely the technical aspect of his or her work, many educators express dissatisfaction at having their work viewed and evaluated only in terms of technical effectiveness (Prillaman, 1988).

Nonetheless, it is not surprising that this technical strand of the discourse on education continues to receive much attention. First, the perspective it promotes is highly compatible with the scientific management style of administration that has governed education, by and large, since the 1940s. More recently, the language of the technical continues to be reinforced by the notions inherent in much of the present school reform movement.

Current notions of reform promote an increased, measurable accountability, which essentially excludes the "something else" that practitioners of education believe to be so essential. It is this something else, what we are calling the *language of the expressive*, which practitioners indicate is left out of the discourse about effective teaching. They express concern and frustration over the implications this technical emphasis has for themselves and their relationships with their students. At present, teacher effectiveness researchers continue to develop more highly technical and standardized methods and theories of teacher effectiveness, accountability, and management. Practitioners themselves, along with other educational researchers, concurrently engage in an alternate conversation: This conversation, composed of the language of the expressive, emphasizes relationships among people within educational contexts.

The Discourse on Caring: The Language of the Expressive

When Gilligan (1982) challenged Kohlberg's work in the early 1980s, her intent was to expand the view of moral development to include a different perspective, that of women. As other writers and researchers reviewed her work, they began to examine the implications of Gilligan's approach, not only for the purposes of understanding moral development, but also for looking at the social structures which produce differences in moral reasoning in men and women.

Gilligan's major theme in her original work, In a Different Voice (1982), was that women see themselves in relation to others rather than in relation to abstract moral principles. Gilligan states that "women's sense of integrity appears to be entwined with an ethic of care, so that to see themselves as women is to see themselves in a relationship of connection" (p. 171). She proposed, at the time of this writing, that an expansion in developmental theory to include adult development along with the then-new theories of women's development "could lead to a changed understanding of human development and a more generative view of human life" (p. 174).

Gilligan continued, in Mapping the Moral Domain (Gilligan et al., 1988), to develop this idea in regard to adolescent development. She describes the ways in which moral structure defined by relationship develops during female adolescence. This work calls into question the cultural definitions of caring as associated with the ideas of female goodness and self-sacrifice. In this work, she cites girls and women who are care-focused thinkers and says

> Care-focused thinkers, primarily but not exclusively girls and women, recognize detachment as morally problematic and underscore the tendency in this highly technological age for people to lose sight of human connection, to overlook the ways in which people enter and affect one another's lives. (p. 290; emphasis added)

In Making Connections (Gilligan et al., 1990), Gilligan, along with Lyons and Hanmer, further develop the work begun in Mapping the Moral Domain by studying the lives of adolescent girls at the Emma Willard School. They discuss the threat of Western culture to adolescent female development and attempt to "change a tradition by including girls' voices, of listening to girls and asking again about the meaning of self, relationship and morality—concepts central to any psychology of human development'' (p. 5).

For our considerations here, the greatest contribution of Gilligan's work was to legitimize the choices of women to make the people and relationships in their lives more important than universal principles and regulations. Further, Gilligan's work supports the moral problem of detachment and highlights the greater need for connection. She suggests that her work has implications for education. However, what is missing is an approach to promoting connection grounded in educational practice.

Nel Noddings (1984), like Gilligan, addresses the issues of disconnection and detachment in Western culture. In *Caring: A Feminine Approach to Ethics and Moral Education* (1984), Noddings describes the perspectives of the ''one caring'' and the one ''cared for'' as a means for developing ''an ethic of caring.'' She asserts that this ethic of caring would better serve as a foundation for society than what has been traditionally called ethics or moral reasoning. Noddings (1986) also speaks directly about what education ought to be doing in regard to an ethic of caring:

> It should, indeed, be our goal in all of education to produce caring, moral persons, but we cannot accomplish this purpose by setting an objective and heading straight toward it. Rather, we approach our goal by living with those whom we teach in a caring community through modeling, dialogue, practice, and confirmation. (p. 502)

Our book is directed at what could be considered the next logical step in the educational goals Noddings describes for developing an ethic of caring. As Noddings suggests, our book explores the work of educational practitioners and their experiences of the modeling, dialogue, and practice, as well as the confirmation they provide in their commitment to care for those in their educational community.

While Gilligan spoke of women's ways of making moral decisions, Belenky et al. (1986) elaborated upon the feminine perspective through their investigation of women's acquisition of knowledge. This work, *Women's Ways of Knowing*, served to further legitimize women's approaches to the world. The authors describe five ways in which women view reality. They point out that while women may have a way of relating to knowledge, truth and authority that is distinct from men's, most educational institutions were founded by men and designed after their own particular way of viewing the world. Further, Belenky et al. go on to describe ways in which educational institutions hinder and help women in their development. For our purposes, however, perhaps the most salient part of *Women's Ways of Knowing* is the discussion of women's families of origin and their influences. It is in their families that socialization begins to shape women's values of caring and relationship. Still, we caution the reader about operating from a masculine and feminine dichotomy.

The works of Gilligan (1982; Gilligan et al., 1988, 1990), Belenky, et al. (1986), and Noddings (1984, 1986) have provided the foundation for the subsequent language of the expressive, the discourse on caring: We suggest that this discourse in education has been either a reaction to, or a building upon, their notions of caring. We propose to expand the discourse by, first, including humankind, rather than just the feminine, in our perceptions of caring. Second, we intend to more richly and fully include the voices of educators for whom caring has been a part of daily practice long before the existence of the academic debate as to its legitimacy.

BEGINNING THE TAPESTRY:
INTERWEAVING THE STRANDS

We will approach our presentation of caring in the educational arena through exploration of the individual strands in the tapestry that we have previously described. We will begin with an examination of the larger cultural contexts that might be seen as the background of the tapestry, or the warp that holds the tapestry together. It is a thread that is ever present—so much so that it becomes virtually unseeable. Interwoven with this background are the multicolored, variable textures that are the experiences of school personnel, administrators, teachers, student teachers, children, higher educators, and researchers.

The first section, entitled "Cultural Perspectives on Caring: From Children and Adults," begins with a chapter by Doris M. Kendrick. She explores the emblematic narratives of two teachers of the handicapped. These narratives, taken from literature, reveal the wider cultural perspectives and ambiguities of caring. In Chapter 2, by Dwight L. Rogers, we are presented with the co-constructed relationship between a fourth grade teacher and her pupils.

Part Two, "Schools: Multiple Manifestations of Caring," includes the stories of a school undergoing change and the role of an administrator. In Chapter 3, Susan Danin examines caring in an elementary school struggling with the implementation of a program for at-risk students. The story of this school clarifies the nature of conflict within caring relationships. These seeming contradictions become apparent in the reactions of school personnel in the context of the school culture. Chapter 4, by Michael Courtney and George Noblit, presents a first-hand account by an elementary school principal of his perceived role as caregiver. The role of principal as caregiver is viewed through the components of caring outlined by Fisher and Tronto (1990)— caring about, taking care of, caregiving, and care-receiving.

"Teachers and Student Teachers: Views of Caregivers," Part 3, presents elements of caring from both ends of the educational spectrum. Van Dempsey, in Chapter 5, looks at the experiences of teachers as they daily grapple with demands for effective teaching and the conflicts that produces in their connections with students. He explores the notions of professionalism in light of these contradictions. In Chapter 6, James McLaughlin describes the process of student teachers learning to care and control. This is an account of how student teachers, in their journey to become teachers, learn to express caring in a way that is functional.

The final section, "Caring From the Ivory Tower: Experiences of Researchers and Professors," steps back to view caring from the perspective of those who are often accused of being distant from the pragmatic considerations of education—higher educators and researchers. Jaci Webb, in Chapter 7, provides evidence which suggests that educational researchers are not removed from the settings they study. This chapter recounts the experience of five researchers, including the author, in their roles as participant observers in a qualitative study of an inner-city elementary school. The author discusses their particular expressions of caring through the ways in which they establish relationships with those in the classrooms they are researching. Finally, in Chapter 8, Deborah Eaker looks at the perspectives on caring from the vantage point of the higher educator, in this case tenured university women. This chapter reveals the commitment to mentoring and empowering of students as well as to personal and social transformation which orient these women to their work and teaching. Their accounts expand the concept of women's expressions of caring to include a sense of personal and social agency.

What is being offered here are particular strands which make up the tapestry of caring within education. We believe that taken as a whole, these varied accounts provide an opening through which we can reconsider our discourse about caring within education. In the final chapter, we will examine the complete tapestry in light of its implications for educational theory and practice.

REFERENCES

Belenky, M. F., Clinchy, B. M., Goldberger, N. R., & Tarule, J. M. (1986). *Women's ways of knowing: The development of self, voice, and mind*. New York: Basic Books.

Bloom, B. S. (1974, September). Time and learning. *American Psychologist*, p. 7.

Brooks, D. M. (1985, Winter). The teacher's communicative competence: The first day of school. *Theory Into Practice*, pp. 63–69.

Duckworth, E. (1985). What teachers know: The best knowledge base. *Harvard Educational Review*, 55(3), 15–17.

Fisher, B., & Tronto, J. (1990). Toward a feminist theory of caring. In E. Abel & M. Nelson (Eds.), *Circles of care*. Albany, NY: SUNY Press.

Gilligan, C. (1982). *In a different voice*. Cambridge, MA: Harvard University Press.

Gilligan, C., Ward, J.V., & Taylor, J.M. (1988). *Mapping the moral domain*. Cambridge, MA: Harvard University Press.

Gilligan, C., Lyons, N. P., & Hanmer, T.J. (1990). *Making connections.* Cambridge, MA: Harvard University Press.

Medley, D. M. (1979). The effectiveness of teachers. In P. Peterson & H. Walberg (Eds.), *Research in teaching: Concepts, findings, and implications.* Berekely, CA: McCutchin.

Noddings, N. (1984). *Caring: A feminine approach to ethics and moral education.* Berkeley, CA: University of California Press.

Noddings, N. (1986). Fidelity in teaching, teacher education, and research for teaching. *Harvard Educational Review, 56*(4), 496–510.

Prillaman, A. R. (1988). *The acquisition of the role identity of teacher.* Unpublished dissertation, University of North Carolina, Chapel Hill.

Rosenshine, B. (1971). *Teaching behaviors and student achievement.* National Foundation for Educational Research in England and Wales.

Part I

Cultural Perspectives on Caring: From Children and Adults

Chapter 1

From Caretaking to Caregiving: Divergent Perspectives Upon Teachers of the Handicapped*

Doris M. Kendrick

FOREGROUND: IMAGES OF PAIN

Like the poor, the disabled are always with us. As the dean of American literary critics, Leslie Fiedler, has warned, their archetypal images, whether "comic, horrific, or pathetic," retain irresistible power to move even the most sophisticated among us "at deep psychic levels" (Fiedler, 1981, p.1). Moving confidently from Shakespeare's malevolent hunchback-king (*Richard III*) to "super-beautiful jockesses" of the modern cinema ("Ice Castles") Fiedler, in his characteristic dual role as *enfant terrible* and literary anthropologist, simultaneously poses—and answers—his real question: What images of the handicapped, because of their enormous and enduring popularity, may therefore be taken as true cultural icons? Critics since Aristotle have agreed with him, "those that arouse in us either pity or fear," those who reveal to us the "primal terrors" that beset even "the most enlightened" beneath our thin veneer of "benign tolerance," those people we secretly regard as "essentially alien, absolute others" (p. 3).

*Portions of this chapter were originally presented at the Tenth Annual Ethnography in Education Research Forum, The University of Pennsylvania, February 1989, as "Icon and Image: Two Emblematic Narratives of Teachers of the Handicapped."

In this chapter I wish, in some sense, to build upon Fiedler's already extensive work, extending my inquiry, however, not further into those disabled "secret selves" we so fear and pity, but rather toward those heretofore unexamined images of their teachers and caregivers, those liminal figures who mediate across a cultural chasm which, we shall see, may be as narrow as a marriage-bed, yet as deep as a deaf-blind child's "still, dark world" (Keller, 1904, p. 16).

Possibly the most salient trait of both the scholarly and popular literature concerning the lives and careers of teachers of the handicapped is that it is essentially nonexistent.[1] Despite the fact that the disabled have become an increasingly visible minority in recent years—witness the perennial popularity of TV's so-called "three-hankie dramas" turning upon that all time most popular misfortune, blindness—their invisible teachers and caregivers remain offstage. Rather, Klobas (1988) has found in her exhaustive survey of film, television, and drama the intrusive presence of a "nondisabled catalyst," an earnest soul who, through heart and will—but no special education or training—is able to restore the handicapped person's self-respect in a "ritualistic formula" that functions as a "charm to ward off the awful reality that everyone is just a slip away from disability" (p. xiii). Oddly enough, the professional literature is equally reticent when limning the character of a teacher of the handicapped, preferring to focus upon "competencies" rather than the whole person. Despite the passage of PL 94–142,[2] legislation that has increasingly "mainstreamed" deaf, blind, emotionally disturbed, and mentally retarded children into classrooms all over America, even *Exceptional Children*, the flagship journal of special education, continues to publish articles that narrowly define a "successful teacher" as "one who has developed a wide range of competencies"—that is,

---

[1]Harlan Lane's massive history of the deaf, for example, lists thirty-two references to "Teachers" but only six of these were published since 1975 and most date from the late nineteenth/early twentieth century. All seem to be narrowly focused studies of teacher-training *methods*; only one, Gallahar, refers to "biographies," but its publication date is 1898.

[2]The "Education of All Handicapped Children" Act; signed November, 1975.

those "skills" needed for the "actual teaching situation" (Scott, 1983, p. 49).[3]

While granting that the "presence of absence" (*pace* Derrida) is ineluctably significant in itself, we turn with some relief from the ephemera of daytime drama and the turgidity of professional prose to an analytic construct borrowed from anthropology, a "blurred genre" flourishing on the boundary between the humanities and the social sciences, often in lightly fictionalized form, but capable of tapping the full range of intellectual and moral resources characteristic of all self-reflective literature.

"Life narrative" is a phrase well known to professional ethnographers from the work of L. L. Langess and Gelya Frank (1981). These and others have pondered the intricate relationship of "life histories" (as they are usually termed) to the culture in which they are embedded, and many have seen "life narrative" as an important form of social reproduction.[4] While these anthropologists have generally taken an oral, interview-based approach to either individuals or groups, I have made it my ongoing task to examine a not-so-familiar subset of their work— "emblematic narrative"—in its text-based avatar of [auto] biography and popular fiction. My particular interest has been to probe the paradoxical "dark side" of the folk-model of the caring teacher in nineteenth-and twentieth-century Anglo-American culture.

These narratives are "emblematic" (a phrase coined, as best I can tell, by anthropologists James Peacock and Dorothy Holland) in the medieval sense of a symbolic "device" or motto. Essentially, they take as their province that liminal space at the intersection of self, text, and culture where persons (or groups) raise their standard to aver, "This is what you must know to know *me*" (Linde, 1980, p. 4).

Because the "voices of fictive characters resound more clearly than those which speak around us" (Cantor & King, 1986, p. 1),

---

[3]It is interesting to note that Scott's article, printed in the journal's 50th anniversary edition, found that practicing teachers of the hearing-impaired rated a knowledge of American Sign Language as their *lowest*-ranked "competency."

[4]*Cf*, for example, Keesing (1985).

short stories, novels, and plays frequently present *via* their
larger-than-life characters ("emblems") those vital—but often
covert— cultural assumptions echoing within a particular time
and place. Popular theater, especially since the mid-thirties, has
presented and endlessly recreated for us powerful and persua-
sive images of pity and fear—or hope and courage—that have
proved irresistibly moving to even the most jaded psyche.[5]

It is to two of these dramaturgical "emblems" of teachers of
the handicapped that I now wish to turn and to more closely
examine throughout the rest of this chapter, probing not only
their evident similarities but also their very real differences—
differences that reflect in a dramatic and unmistakable fashion
that our cultural perspectives upon caring teachers seem to have
diverged significantly in the space of a single generation.[6]

MIDDLE DISTANCE: EMBLEMS OF CARE

Frame One: a sophisticated Broadway audience is riveted by the
ferocity and power of the struggle between a wild deaf-
blind-mute child and a wry young teacher of the handicapped.
Based upon the life stories of actual people and sparsely staged,
the play is frankly a documentary; but the "Homeric grap-
plings" between the two protagonists build to a wrenching
climax that more than one critic will call "unforgettable theater"
("Newsweek," 11/2/59, p. 97). The award-winning stage play is
quickly adapted as a successful motion picture marked by

---

[5]Very seldom however will any teacher receive full-scale novelistic treatment in his/her role strictly as an educator. Those rare and relatively brief
instances are almost always based upon the life and work of an actual person
known to the author. The prime example is that quintessential portrait of the
lovable British schoolmaster, *Goodbye, Mr. Chips*, closely modelled upon
James Hilton's own schoolmaster-father.

[6]*Cf.* Holland, D. C., and Quinn, N. (Eds.) (1987). *Cultural Models in
Language and Thought*. New York: Cambridge University Press and Peacock,
J. L. and Tyson, R. W. 1986. "Wesleyan and Calvinist Narrations of Life
Story." Paper presented April 27, 1986, at Southern Anthropological Society
Meeting, session on Life Histories and Cultural Models.

arresting visual imagery and "electrifying" performances from the two leads. Awards and honors are heaped upon all involved.

Frame Two: a glittering New York theater crowd is stunned by the fragile beauty and raw anger of a deaf-mute student engaged in intimate battle with a wisecracking young teacher of the handicapped. Based in part upon the events in the life of a deaf-mute person well known to the playwright, the brief play is staged with minimalist sets, and its action occurs in an extended flashback as the characters step forward from the teacher's memory and speak to the audience. The climactic confrontation between the two protagonists leaves the audience exhausted but applauding wildly. After a successful run, the play is made into a movie that critics find "visually stunning" (Schickel, 1986, p. 95). Like the drama, it will reap a harvest of accolades and prizes for director, actors, and screenplay.

These two classics of the modern theater are, of course, *The Miracle Worker* by William Gibson (1960) and *Children of a Lesser God* by Mark Medoff (1980). In both the real-life person of Annie Sullivan and the fictional character of James Leeds we find enormously moving portrayals of what contemporary American culture holds a dedicated and caring teacher to be, particularly a teacher who must minister to the needs of the deaf and blind. But because the concept of "caring" itself is endlessly complex, inherently unstable, subject to change over time, and inevitably grounded not only in each person's but every culture's own contextual experience of relationship—what Noddings calls "natural caring" (1980)—our evolving folk-images of contemporary teachers and caregivers must needs, over time, diverge and develop as well. The sociocultural role of teacher of the handicapped, moreover, offers us a rare perspective upon the caring act as it is embodied and contested in the daily arena of education, for here a shared understanding between the "one-caring" and "one-cared-for" cannot simply be assumed. Sometimes even the most elemental forms of communication are difficult to establish across a gulf of silence and darkness; and, because of the uneven nature of the power nexus in this particular teacher–student relationship, the potential for abuse of that power is ever-present.

And it is here we find that language itself, the very words we use every day to talk about caring, has faithfully preserved for use—just below the level of consciousness perhaps—subtle but vital distinctions between a pair of cognates that can both clarify our perspective and focus our inquiry.

Our modern English word "care," which ultimately derives from the ancient Indo-European root * GAR, ("to cry out") is in itself fraught with double meaning, having (via the Anglo-Saxon "caru") a nominative sense of care as "burden" or "sorrow" but also, as a verb or participle, the more common sense of "liking; to hold in high regard; heed; and protection," (from the Latin carus, which has given us the now somewhat archaic English word "charity"). Thus we may and readily do distinguish—consciously or not—between "care taking" and "care giving."

"Caretaking" inevitably implies, in Noddings' phrase, "an unequal relationship," one with no possibility of ever achieving full reciprocity between the One-caring and the One-cared-for. Caretaking generally connotes conscientious custodial care, as of pets or buildings-and-grounds, or—perhaps at best—tender, but essentially limited, attention to the bodily needs of the equally helpless very young or very old. Although this sort of caring may entail much "moral good," as in "taking care" of the environment, Noddings (p. 158–9) argues that because no truly responsive relationship can ever be established, what is really playing upon the heart and mind of the One-caring is only "affection" or "sentiment," a notion that will move the One-caring "steadily away from the ethical toward the [merely] sensitive and aesthetic" (p. 161).

"Caregiving," on the other hand—and we instinctively sense this—taps the hidden semantic depths: the One-caring "hears" the chthonic "cry" and answers that voice; the One-cared-for acknowledges and freely responds in turn (p. 72–3), thus completing and replicating those spiraling "chains of caring" throughout a society, a culture, a world.

Professor Fiedler reminds us that "not until the rise of sentimentalism and the obsession with the excluded and the marginal which climaxed in the reign of Victoria did the blind, the deaf, and the halt become major characters in large numbers of books . . . " (p. 2). And of all these pathetic characters, no one embodied more heroically the images of pity, fear, hope, and courage than Helen Keller, that "living prototype of popular novels of the late Victorian era—isolated, intelligent, brave, and tragic" (Klobas, p.1). Anyone, then, concerned with the origins of modern iconic portraiture of the caring teacher must begin with Keller's mentor, Annie Sullivan Macy, for if Helen Keller became a living legend, a "miracle child," then the "miracle worker" herself achieved near-mythic stature during her own lifetime. Even a century later, Sullivan remains the unchallenged "hallmark of the dedicated teacher" (Lash, 1980, p.373) for an admiring world.

But as emblem of her essential care *taker* role we have preserved for us, in a carefully posed photograph, the canonical representation of the "rapt, golden Helen" who appears to be listening expectantly, while "Teacher," a dark woman of "increasingly Falstaffian girth," peers intently down at her own wondrous creation.[7] Their hands are, as always, firmly clasped in this familiar yet arresting image of the caretaker-teacher who—quite literally—held the hand of her only pupil until the day she died.

Yet, from Sullivan's early letters published in an appendix to Keller's *The Story of My Life* (1904) and the biographical work of Nella Braddy Henny (1933), emerges the portrait not of a custodian but of a genuine educator: bold, largely self-taught, always ready to trust her own instincts, a risk-taker, but steadfast and determined at all times to will the child's best interests; humorous, self-deprecating, and tough-minded; full of compassion but no obvious pity for the blighted Helen. It is their shared tragedy, then, that Sullivan's and Keller's "emblem" eventually coalesced and hardened into the lifelong symbiosis we see validated in *The Miracle Worker*, wherein the teacher-as-caretaker promises to stay "forever and ever."

As the lights come up about midway through Act I, we meet the young Annie Sullivan of Gibson's vision. She is full of

---

[7]This emblematic photograph was taken in July of 1894 at the home of Alexander Graham Bell, when Helen was 14 and Sullivan was 28; a slightly cropped version appears on the cover of Lash's dual biography of Keller and Sullivan.

"crude vitality," though nearly blind herself and thoroughly inept with Helen's genteel Southern family; she impatiently wrests her bulky suitcase away from the appalled Captain Keller: "I've got something in it for Helen!" But a darker strain is added to this stereotype of the "spunky Irish lass" with a voiceover from the past "It hurts. Annie, it hurts . . . Annie, when are we goin' home? . . . Forever and ever, you said forever" (Act I).

Although in real life Sullivan waited 40 years before she told Keller of the Dickensian horrors of her childhood in the Tewksbury Poorhouse and her younger brother's death there, in the play we find her using this startling revelation as something of a weapon to get total, daily control of Helen: "I grew up in an asylum. The state almshouse . . . it made me strong."

The theme of "total control" will emerge in the subsequent action of the play as Sullivan's main educational tactic for civilizing the feral Helen and effecting the "miracle" itself—the gift of language that will enable her to break out of her "steel cell" of darkness and silence:

> I want complete charge of her . . . I mean night and day. She has to be dependent on me [for] oh . . . everything. The food she eats, the clothes she wears, fresh air, yes, the air she breathes, whatever her body needs is a primer to teach her out of. It's the only way: the one who lets her have it should be her teacher.

In Act III, as the plot spirals into the climactic scene at the pump, Sullivan demands: "Let me keep her to what she has learned, and she'll go on learning from me. Take her out of my hands and it all comes apart."

While we shall return to Helen's epiphany in the wellhouse with the "water of life" on her palms, out of which she is literally "reborn" as a fully aware, fully human creature, the most revealing piece of stagecraft in the entire play actually occurs in the denouement. Gibson's written directions underscore that Helen, in "their first act of verbal communication," spells out a single word into her mother's hand: "and she [Mrs. Keller] can hardly utter the word aloud, in wonder, gratitude, and deprivation; it is a moment in which she simultaneously finds and loses a child." That momentous word is, of course, "Teacher." The curtain falls with the iconic dyad indelibly fixed: Helen and Teacher, hand in hand— "forever and ever."[8]

Moving forward a generation to the fictional character of James Leeds, we find in Medoff's work a very different sort of emblem for teachers of the handicapped, one that much more closely approximates the image of teacher as care giver. But even here there will be contradictions within caring—a "dark side" adumbrated by the play's title, which excerpts a phrase from Tennyson's "Idylls of the King": "For why is all around us here, As if some lesser god had made the world, But had not force to shape it as he would?" Far from being a "miracle worker," Leeds will discover as the play unfolds that he, too, is as much a "child of a lesser god" as the young deaf and deaf-mute residents of the school where he has come to teach; and that, for all his dedication and depth of caring, he will "lack the force to shape" even the most intimate of his relationships "as he would."

While Gibson could assume widespread cultural awareness and warm acceptance of the story of Sullivan and Keller, Medoff seems to have quite consciously set out to create a new emblem for teachers of the handicapped, one that would better reflect society's post-Civil Rights Movement images of the disabled themselves. In a preface to the play entitled "Not So Random Notes from the Playwright," he tells of meeting Phyllis Frelich, an enormously impressive deaf-mute actress, and finding her "irresistible . . . honest . . . fiercely full of life and love" (p. 2). Medoff immediately committed himself to writing a play expressly for Frelich, who won a Tony for her portrayal of Sarah, the deaf-mute protagonist opposite Leeds, in the original Broadway version of the play. Medoff also offers some insight into his specific dramatic intent:

Though it is Sarah who most interests me, the play is more about James. . . . I (in my head) have been James for as long as there has

---

[8]Keller was still alive at the time of the writing of this play, and Gibson made much of consulting her for background information; yet his final script, while considered bold and innovative by the standards of the time, relies almost exclusively upon Sullivan's early letters rather than Keller's personal memories. Although Gibson professed to be "enamored" of Sullivan, Keller herself disliked the play because it presented "too coarse" a portrait of her beloved Teacher.

been a James. . . . For the first time in my writing career I want to create fully sympathetic characters . . . (p. 6).

He continues:

> We are quite a hit in L. A. Audiences laugh and cry. They like these people and are moved by their lives. They are also conscious, I think, of being present at the birth of a historical undertaking. Though I never sat around and wondered why it hadn't been done before, certainly I am mindful of the newness of this play's concept, and Gordon [the director] has all along urged me to find the essential moments, scenes, ideas that make the relationship of James and Sarah unique(p. 6–7).

Before proceeding further, perhaps a brief synopsis of the plot is in order. James Leeds (almost surely a pun on "leads"), an energetic and irreverent young speech therapist, arrives at a state school for deaf children and teenagers. The audience immediately senses that he will be successful with the students because of his self-mocking humor, offbeat classroom antics, resistance to authority, and obvious dedication to the difficult task of teaching young people to articulate sounds that they themselves cannot hear. He abruptly encounters and quickly falls in love with the beautiful, brilliant, angry Sarah, a former student now working as a maid at the school because her refusal to communicate in any medium other than American Sign Language has closed her off from either further education or meaningful, well-paid work. Although James and Sarah become first lovers and eventually husband and wife, it is not the strong erotic element of their relationship that dominates the action of the play. Rather, it is their multifaceted struggle for dominance, as symbolized by James' insistence that Sarah learn from him to speak aloud, instead of depending solely upon signing, that drives the plot to the rending climax that both begins and ends the play:

> Sarah (Signing): Me have nothing. Me deafy. Speech inept. Intelligence—tiny blockhead. English—blow away. Left one you. Depend—no. Think myself enough. Join, unjoined. (In standard English: I

have nothing; no hearing, no speech, no intelligence, no language. I have only you. I don't
need you. I have me alone. Join, unjoined.)

James (Aloud): She went away from me. Or did I drive her
away? I don't know.

All of the action of the play focuses upon James's repeated
attempt to answer this tragic question. Ultimately, he will come
to see that his insistence upon maintaining an inappropriate
teacher role—as a caretaker rather than a caregiver—has destroyed his relationship with the proud, independent Sarah. The
irony of James's situation is heightened in that he is, in fact, an
excellent teacher. Endlessly patient, he works with the hostile
Orin:

Orin: Santiona.

James: Wait, please. Watch. Sanction. Un. Un.

Orin: Santiona. That was wrong, damn it!

James: That's okay, Orin. . . . Watch my mouth. Cut it. Sanction.
Look in here. Sanction. "Un." (Indicating the movement
of the tongue to the roof of the mouth.)

Orin: Sanction.

James: Yes! Good for you. How did that feel?

Orin: How did it sound?

James: It sounded beautiful.

Orin: Then it felt all right.

James: Speech.

Orin: Speech. [Act 1]

Even in the face of Sarah's jealous taunts of the insecure Lydia,
James attempts to be supportive of the younger student:

Lydia: Can I watch your new TV?

Sarah: Watch in the TV lounge.

Lydia: I don't like to watch in the TV lounge. You always have to
keep changing the volume on your hearing aid. Everyone
is always fighting about how loud the sound should be.

> Yesterday, I almost had a nervous breakdown. I did.
> Really. (To James, when Sarah appears unmoved) Mr.
> Leeds. . . .

Leeds: Oh, come on, Sarah, let her watch your TV. It's good for
her—she picks up the pronunciation of words.

Sarah: Fine. Go. Watch TV.

Lydia: Yay! [Act II]

But so much of James's sense of self has been mistakenly
invested in the "total caretaker" role that he is unable to step
outside it. Increasingly obsessed with teaching Sarah to speak
aloud, he finally pushes her to a shrieking, barely understandable fury:

> Sarah (Aloud): Speech! Speech! Is that it? No! You want me to be
> your child! You want me to be like you. How do
> you like my voice? Am I beautiful? Am I what
> you want me to be? What about me? What I want?
> What I want!

In a mirror-image of Helen and Teacher's "miracle" of union
at the pump, James and Sarah's equally violent confrontation
rips them apart; and it is the teacher, not the pupil, who achieves
the greater growth through painful self-knowledge:

> Yes, I am a terrific teacher: Grow, Sarah, but not too much.
> Understand yourself, but not better than I understand you. Be
> brave, but not so brave you don't need me anymore. Your silence
> frightens me. When I'm in that silence, I hear nothing, I feel like
> nothing. I can never pull you into my world of sound any more
> than you can open some magic door and bring me into your
> silence. I can say that now.

In the final scene, the lights fade slowly down upon Sarah's
graceful hand-held gesture of "join," hinting of a future recon-
ciliation; but for the present, James is bereft of wife and pupil
and wrenchingly aware that care must be given and received,
but never taken: "You just don't have the right to demand that
anyone be created in your image."

BACKDROP: ICONS OF POWER

It is all but impossible in this brief chapter to attempt much more than a simple offering-up of these powerful and paradoxical images of care for the beginning of an academic discourse. I would, however, at least like to open the dialogue with two specific "lessons" I believe that these emblems of Sullivan and Leeds, both as caretakers and caregivers, have to teach us about what the greater culture understands the truly caring teacher to be.

The first is that care *taking* inevitably becomes demonic—in the classic sense of "possessed"—when the recipient of that care, however disabled, is a fully aware, fully rational, fully responsive human being: Both teacher and student will eventually find themselves "possessed" by the relationship itself. Locked into each other's inescapable embrace, their freedom and their reciprocity—that "major intrinsic reward of teaching" (Noddings, p. 73)—will be forfeit. Noddings quotes Buber: "Relation[ship] *is* reciprocity" and goes on to underscore that freedom, creativity, and a "happy growth" comprise that "genuine reciprocity" that "serves to prevent the caring from turning back on the One-caring in the form of anguish and concern for self" (p. 74). Yet we now know that this was precisely Sullivan's fate, inasmuch as she could never bring herself to relinquish the role of teacher-as-caretaker to Helen, who—however loving, kind, and spontaneous her temperament may indeed have been—was thereby denied not only any sort of meaningful growth and personal freedom, but also that "special reciprocity that connotes completion" (p. 151).

No less astute observer of human nature than Mark Twain sensed this fatal grip and exclaimed upon meeting Helen Keller: "You are a wonderful creature, *you and your other half together*—Miss Sullivan, I mean—for it took the pair of you to make a complete and perfect whole" (Lash, p. 474, emphasis added).

Bruno Bettelheim (1980) has suggested that the power Sullivan can still exert over our collective imagination is the "illusion" we see so skillfully recreated in the "miracle" of Helen herself: that one may be blind, deaf, and mute and yet be happy; that somewhere, somehow, each handicapped person will reap a wonderful, caring Teacher, exorcising thereby those lurking images of pity and fear, while further assuaging the greater culture's sense of guilt over the desperate plight of the disabled.

But when we step outside the world-under-glass of *The Miracle Worker*, we are reminded that the price paid by the caretaker was immense: a brief, failed marriage; nagging illness and the eventual loss of her eyesight; then a final, tortured descent into delusions, dementia, and death. (Braddy, 1933; Lash, 1980). And from Lash's recent work with previously unpublished materials come further revelations only whispered while Sullivan yet lived: that, despite surface acquiescence, she adamantly and successfully blocked Helen's attempts to speak clearly—lest she become independent of Teacher—and ruthlessly destroyed Keller's single intimate relationship with a young man who had hoped to marry her.[9] In her last years, though obviously failing, Sullivan stubbornly refused to adequately train Miss Polly Thomson, her designated successor, so that, upon Teacher's death, Helen was left with a companion who was totally unprepared for the rigors of Teacher's caretaker role. Polly also succumbed rather rapidly to stress-related disorders, and a truncated Keller spent the remaining years of her long life essentially and horribly alone in her "steel cell" of darkness and silence.[10]

The second lesson that these emblematic teachers would have us learn is that while there now seems to be considerable consensus that the teacher-as-care*taker* is no longer an adequate

---

[9]Lash recounts at some length this tragic episode that occurred in the fall of 1916 as "Helen in Love," pp. 435–449. Much earlier, however, in 1897, when Dr. Arthur Gilman (head of the Cambridge School for Young Ladies) had attempted to separate Sullivan from Keller for instructional purposes, Teacher wrote, outraged: "I have given Helen all that I had to give—myself, my service, my love; and she has given me in return the tenderest love in the world. . . . All the powers on Earth cannot separate Helen and me" (p. 227–8). And, even more chillingly, "It is not a teacher that the deaf-blind want; it is another self . . . (p. 205).

[10]The phrase "steel cell" was evidently coined by Will Cressy, a New York columnist and keen observer of Keller when she performed on the vaudeville circuit. Over the years, many others have also applied it to her plight; it is quoted numerous times by Lash, pp. 494–5.

model, neither will a simplistic "progression" to the teacher-as-caregiver successfully bridge the chasm that separates us from those disabled persons whom we perceive to be the very essence of "Otherness"; rather, the "Others" themselves must reach out to us with their own freely offered gestures of reciprocity and love.

The mechanism whereby new images of hope and courage will replace the ancient ones of pity and fear is *empowerment*, and the truly *caregiving* teacher will embody the role of mediator of that power for good on behalf of the culture at large.

Biographers, novelists, and playwrights have not only instinctively sensed the potential power of the caring teacher —for good or for evil—they also have consciously patterned that awareness into the very language of their texts. In the two plays that we have considered here, both Gibson and Medoff have purposely chosen—one might even say have been driven to choose—heightened religious imagery in order to adequately reinforce the heavy metaphoric weight of this great "lesson": Sullivan, like Jesus of Nazareth, is a worker of miracles, including even the greatest of all:—she has literally "called forth Lazarus" in the restoration to fully human life through the power of the gift of language to what had been an isolated and feral child. In Keller's own account of the "miracle at the pump":

> Suddenly I felt a misty consciousness as of something forgotten—
> a thrill of returning thought. . . . I knew then that "w-a-t-e-r"
> meant the wonderful cool something that was flowing over my
> hand. That living word awakened my soul, gave it light, hope,
> joy, set it free! . . . I learned a great many new words that day. I
> do not remember what they all were, but I do know that mother,
> father, sister, teacher were among them—words that were to make
> the world blossom for me, "like Aaron's rod, with flowers"
> (Keller, pp. 16–17).

As a reflection of the pervasive loss of traditional faith in a more humanistically oriented age, Medoff has largely eschewed overtly Judeo-Christian imagery, preferring instead to ring subtle changes upon the veiled and quasi-pagan trope of Tennyson's "lesser god" whose creative "force" has been found somewhat lacking.[11] "Yet because Leeds has been forced to confront not only his very real limits as a teacher but also the potential of even care giving for misuse of that power, a liminal space between teacher and student has been opened up. Though there will be for him "no sign from Heaven," he may reach out his hand as an equal to his wife and pupil, who, as proxy for all those handicapped others, can creatively and in freedom offer (at least the possibility) of her own in return.

Victor Turner has argued that "A drama is never really complete . . . until it is performed, that is, acted on some kind of stage before an audience. A theatrical audience sees the material of real life presented in meaningful form" (Turner, 1986, p. 27).

The final emblematic meaning of the teacher-as-caregiver, then, must be endlessly re-enacted in the arena of real life as power-*for* not power-*over*:

| James: | I think . . . I dream . . . And in my dream I see her coming back to me with one last note . . . it is written in space with her two hands. It says |
| James and Sarah: | (signing and speaking) I'll help you if you'll help me. |

REFERENCES

Bettelheim, B. (August 4, 1980). Review of *Helen and Teacher: The Story of Helen Keller and Anne Sullivan Macy. The New Yorker, 56,* 85–90.

Braddy, N. H. (1933). *Anne Sullivan Macy.* Garden City, NY: Doubleday Doran.

Cantor, N. F., & King, N. (Eds.). (1986). *Notebooks in Cultural Analysis, An Annual Review,* Vol. 3. A special issue on "Voice." Durham, NC: Duke University Press.

Fiedler, L. A. (1982). "Pity and fear: Images of the disabled in literature and the popular arts." In *Proceedings of the International Center for the Disabled Literary Symposium* in collaboration with the United Nations (October 27,

---

[11]Strangely enough the title of the play has been widely misunderstood, even by critics, as a slur upon members of the American deaf subculture, who— quite to the contrary—consider this drama to be their "morality play" and the "most important artistic event ever experienced by the deaf community" (Neisser, 1983, p. 262).

1981). An edited transcript of this conference appeared in *Salmagundi*, Number 57.

Hilton, J. R. (1934, 1962). *Goodbye, Mr. Chips*. Boston: Little, Brown and Co.

Keller, H. A. (1990). *The story of my life*. New York: Bantam Books.

Keesing, R. (1985). Kwiao women speak: The Micropolitics of autobiography in a Solomon Island society. *American Anthropologist 87*, 27–39.

Klobas, L. E. (1988). *Disability drama in television and film*. Jefferson, NC, and London: McFarland and Co., Inc.

Lane, H. (1984). *When the mind hears: A history of the deaf*. New York: Random House.

Langess, L. L., and Frank, G. (1981). *Lives: An anthropological approach to biography*. Novato, California: Chandler and Sharp.

Lash, J. P. (1980). *Helen and Teacher: The story of Helen Keller and Anne Sullivan Macy*. Radcliffe Biography Series. New York: Delacorte Press.

Linde, C. (1982, May). The life-story: A temporally discontinuous discourse type. Paper presented at Folk Models Conference, Princeton Institute for Advanced Study.

Medoff, M. (1980). *Children of a lesser god: A play in two acts*. Salt Lake City, UT: Peregrine Smith Books.

Neisser, A. (1983). *The other side of silence: Sign language and the deaf community in America*. New York: Alfred A. Knopf.

New Plays on Broadway [Unsigned review.] *Newsweek*, November 2, 1959. 54:97.

Noddings, N. (1984). *Caring: A feminine approach to ethics and morality*. Berkeley and Los Angeles: University of California Press.

Schickel, R. (1986, October 20). Untitled review, *Time*, p. 95.

Scott, P. L. (1983). Have competencies needed by teachers of the hearing impaired changed in twenty-five years? *Exceptional Children 50*(1), 4–54.

Turner, V. (1986). Images and reflections: Ritual, drama, carnival, film, and spectacle in cultural performance. In *The Anthropology of Performance* (pp. 21–32). New York: PAJ.

Chapter 2

Conceptions of Caring in a Fourth-Grade Classroom*

Dwight L. Rogers

When we think of caring, we usually think of gentle smiles and warm hugs. However, caring may be expressed in a multitude of different ways. As Noddings (1992) suggests:

> Caring cannot be achieved by formula. It requires address and response; it requires different behaviors from situation to situation and person to person. It sometimes calls for toughness, sometimes tenderness. With cool, formal people, we respond caringly with deference and respect; with warm informal people, we respond caringly with hugs and overt affection. Some situations require only a few minutes of attentive care; others require continuous effort over long periods of time (p. i)

It was with the understanding that caring is both situation and person specific that I sought to better understand one teacher's and her students' perception of caring in school.

From early September 1989 until early June 1990, I spent one day each week in a fourth-grade classroom in an inner-city school in the Southeast. The school serves a mixed-race (African-American and white) student population from middle to lower

*This work was supported by a grant from the Lilly Endowment Program on Youth and Caring

income homes. My role as researcher evolved, growing from that of a socially detached observer, to a mildly involved participant observer, to a true participant observer in the spring, when I acted as a teaching assistant and tutor. In April, I administered an open-ended questionnaire to the 26 children in the class, following up their brief responses with three sets of 10- to 20-minute, one-on-one interviews in May and June. The questionnaire and follow-up interview focused on the children's feelings about school and their teachers. I also formally interviewed Martha Duncan (a pseudonym), the teacher in this classroom, on five occasions—in October, January, April, May, and June. In two of the interviews, I asked her the questions from the children's questionnaire. During my other interviews with Martha, I asked her a variety of questions related to her classroom, her teaching, and her students. The descriptions and interpretations below derive from the information found in my fieldnotes and the teacher's and children's responses to the questionnaire, interviews, and informal discussions.

As Noddings (1992) suggests above, the act of caring for another is person and situation specific. Through my analysis and interpretation of the information collected from this teacher and these children, however, some themes—and variations on themes—of caring in this fourth-grade classroom have emerged. By piecing together the teacher's and children's actions and words, I began to get a picture (albeit an incomplete one) of their perceptions of caring and how caring was co-constructed by the participants in this classroom.

THE CHILDREN'S CONCEPTIONS
OF A CARING TEACHER

The power of the spoken word is illustrated time and again in children's responses to questions asking them how their teachers show them that they care. According to Alisha, "All the things that teachers do to show you that they care sort of tie into talking to you." Teachers do not necessarily tell children directly that they care for them, but instead let them know indirectly through their comments. This talk takes a variety of forms depending upon the child and the situation. Simple words of recognition and praise ("Great job!"), or encouragement and advice ("You're doing good! But you need to improve a little bit.") appear to be especially meaningful to these children. These, of course, are comments that all good teachers typically make to their students. I mention them not because of their novelty, but because of the great importance they seem to hold for the children. For, as Margaret explains, "sometimes it's just little things" that teachers do or say that show they care. These children's responses emphasize the critical nature of the brief, almost fleeting, interpersonal interactions teachers have with their students in schools day after day (Noddings, 1986, 1992).

In addition to teachers making brief personal comments to them, some of the children also feel that caring teachers are those who take time (a rare commodity in classrooms) to listen carefully and talk to them one-to-one about their "problems." These problems mostly entail fights with friends, difficulty with schoolwork, and negative experiences at home. In many of the children's minds, a caring teacher is not only someone who tells them when they are doing something well but is also open and willing to listen to them (Lyons, 1983). Caring "talk" is recip- rocal (Richert, 1987). Christine said that caring teachers are those who are open and approachable and who say to children "don't be afraid to tell me whatever."

Janie Ward (1990) defines caring as "responding to another in his or her own terms." The children's use of the word under- stand seems to be much in this same vein. Alisha expresses what appears to be a prevalent belief of the other children regarding how a teacher cares: "Well, they try to understand. Understand what you do. Understand the attitude of different kinds of work. Try to give you work that fits your personality." These children believe that a caring teacher is someone who tries to see things from their perspective, who is both empathetic and sympathetic. According to Andrew, a teacher exhibits care and understanding when she "takes it easy on you when you're in a bad mood." Patricia believes a caring teacher is highly empathetic and helps you and will not "embarrass you by asking you something you don't know." In other words, a caring teacher meets children "where they are," on their own terms (Belenky, Clinchy, Goldberger, & Tarule, 1986).

Over half of the class believes a caring teacher is someone who protects you, someone who "makes sure you don't get hurt" and "won't let nobody hurt you or nothing." Some of the children feel that a teacher who did not care would say things to them like, "So what? Who cares?" if they were hurt. They believe, if a child gets into a fight, that an uncaring teacher "don't do nothing about it. They let you fight."

Few replies carried as intense an emotional response as when the children talked about the importance of teachers keeping them from getting hurt or coming to their aid after they were hurt. It appears, however, that the children are not so concerned about the pain and suffering associated with injury but want their teacher to exhibit concern for them as an individual. Their apparent need to be protected from bodily harm seems to be eclipsed by an even greater need for their teacher to attend, comfort, and recognize them after an injury.

Many of the children feel a caring teacher is a teacher who gives you a "second chance," the opportunity to make mistakes and then learn from them, a chance to do something over again, to get a fresh start. The children are also extremely concerned about teachers being "fair." Fairness is especially critical in relation to not being blamed for the misbehavior of others. There is a strong concern among these children that each child be treated justly, not necessarily equally, which also means that every child must be given an equitable (again, not necessarily equal) amount of the teacher's time and attention. Finally, many of the children believe that caring teachers make school "fun," not "boring," by providing them with interesting and meaningful activities, along with the chance to do "special things" and not "going straight through the book."

The image that emerges from these children's perceptions of a caring teacher is that of a highly responsive individual whose words and actions seem to invite children to communicate: a person who is sensitive to the children's needs and able to understand things from their perspective; a just human being who seeks connection with his or her students; a person who is confident enough to let his or her students make mistakes and give them another chance. A caring teacher, finally, is somebody who is willing to take chances and design and implement an interesting curriculum while providing a safe and secure environment for learning.

As Noddings (1992) clearly states, caring is not something to be accomplished by "formula." We cannot and should not offer a model of a caring classroom for other teachers to attempt to replicate in order to ensure that caring occurs in their own classes. Caring is always a situation- and person-specific act. These children's ideas about what constitutes a caring teacher, however, can provide us with some suggestions for how we may think about caring for all children in our nation's schools. The collection of these ideas is not a prescription to be meticulously followed but instead represents a collage of children's conceptions of caring, which may be carefully studied as a range of possibilities for teachers to reflect upon and to consider in their strivings for connection and caring for children.

THE TEACHER'S BELIEFS ABOUT CARING

These children's teacher, Martha Duncan, believes a caring teacher is "warm, perceptive, open, and honest with the kids and willing to talk about whatever needs to be talked about." She thinks that teachers who care are "easier to develop warm relationships with, because they are more approachable." According to Martha, children show they care with:

> Some real obvious things, like giving you hugs or patting you on the back or noticing that your—I mean a lot of the same things you do for kids. Notice your hair is different, that you got a new pair of shoes. Writing you love letters. I think they demonstrate that they care about the relationship between the two of you by trying.

Responsibility And Caring

Martha, like Noddings (1986), believes that "every child can learn," and it is the "responsibility of the teacher to reach each

child.'' She defines a good teacher as ''someone who is genuinely concerned about what happens to the kids . . . I think a
good teacher helps kids to be curious about things. Helps kids
learn how to learn.'' She is relentless to the point of stubborn-
ness in her pursuit of helping children become more competent,
both socially and academically. She says:

> I have a tendency not to give up on anybody, it's the challenge of
> it. I truly don't believe that there is a child that can't learn. I think
> they will learn in different ways, at different paces. There's got to
> be a way to get to or through to every child. . . . It is my
> responsibility to find it . . . to provide the best situation for
> everybody or provide a way in which everybody can learn what
> they need to learn. So that's part of what keeps me going. I think
> part of it is just the challenge of solving the puzzle.

This persistence is a hallmark of her teaching and is driven by
her strong belief in the possibilities of formal education to
provide the foundation for a meaningful future. It is telling that
Martha ''doesn't like it when kids can't dream.''

Martha thinks, when a teacher says a child ''just doesn't
care,'' that ''it's probably a child who doesn't do, in the
classroom, what all the children are supposed to do,'' and that
this is a child that the teacher has not ''established a relationship
with.'' She firmly states, ''I don't think there is a kid who
doesn't care. If they have a real lackadaisical attitude, I think it's
a defense more than anything else.'' Martha feels that caring for
children is not *just* a nice thing to do, it is a teacher's ethical
responsibility to care. According to her, the children:

> Come the first day trusting that you are going to do the right thing
> for them. They're ready to love you . . . they're really generous
> with their affection and they give it freely without too much
> introspection. . . . They're real forgiving . . . so teachers bear the
> responsibility when taking care of that trust and letting them
> know it is reciprocal.

Creating Opportunities To Care

Martha reciprocates children's trust in a variety of ways. Conversation plays a critical role in the everyday workings of this

classroom. Conversations among children and teacher–child dialogues are the most common forms of interaction in the class. The children sit at rectangular tables in groups of four to six. The group composition often changes, but peer interaction is encouraged in almost every activity except during the occasional teacher-directed lessons. The children are free to communicate at a reasonable noise level and are encouraged to help each other with problems they may encounter in their assignments. This peer assistance and communication occurs both informally and through formally planned cooperative learning activities.

Martha spends much of the day working with individual students. These interactions are often brief and usually center around helping children with occasional difficulties in the class assignments. However, in those few minutes, Martha appears to give that student her full, undivided attention. In addition to the short conversations that occur in the classroom during the school day, Martha also has individual "conferences" when no other children are around. She describes these conferences as:

> Just a more formal way of doing things that happen informally a lot, except that it is more intense. . . . It serves a lot of different purposes. It gives the kids some one-to-one special attention that's usually uninterrupted. It's about something that one or both of us think is very important. It's a chance to talk through a problem and arrive at some sort of agreement as to what's going to happen next. And you are sort of making a commitment through each of you saying, "I'm going to help you do this and here's what you can do to help me help you do this." I think it strengthens the bond between the two of you.

In addition to individual conferences, Martha also convenes class meetings. These meetings are called on special occasions:

> Because of an event I feel the whole class needs to deal with as a group, or because, emotionally, things seem to be reaching an out-of-control point. Class meetings sort of clear the air, and the kids sometimes feel silly. It makes them laugh. It relieves the tension that has built up and gives them a chance to say what they need to say, within certain parameters. I think it gives the kids a

feeling that what they have to say is important and that together, as a group, we want to solve this problem and make a decision.

Martha eats her lunch with the children so that she can engage in longer, more involved conversations with them. She loves these lunchtime dialogues because the children:

Tell you about themselves, and you treat that as something worth listening to. . . . It's a way to discover common interests. Like, Jeremy loves to garden and I like to garden, so we had things we could talk about all year long. . . . I think those are the kind of things that make a relationship with a kid extra special.

She also likes these lunchroom conversations because they provide her with the chance to interact with the children on a different level. According to Martha:

It's one time in the day where it is relaxed and the conversation has nothing to do with school. So it is a whole different kind of— it's a different part of the relationship. We talk about birthdays and families, T.V., dreams, and lies. It's just very different. It is much more casual and informal. It's much less like a teacher–student kind of relationship and more like friends sitting around talking about whatever you feel like talking about.

Martha feels the chance to become more personal with her students through informal conversation is especially important to her teaching (Belenky et al., 1986).

As a teacher, she also feels it is important for her to build a sense of community, to "create a group that kids feel they belong to," and that the children feel as if there are real people in the group "who care about them and they can trust." Martha believes "kids need to feel they belong, have roots, that someone is looking out for their best interests and always cares about who you are and what you need and want." Teacher–child conversations and peer dialogue encourage a sense of trust and provide the glue that connects these kids together with each other and with their teacher (Lyons, 1983).

It's also necessary, however, that the children feel good about themselves in order for genuine dialogue to take place. Martha tries to encourage the development of a positive self-image in her students through a variety of ways. Humor, laughter, and fun are an integral part of this classroom. She establishes a classroom climate in which children are allowed to express their individuality, yet must also respect the individuality of others:

> Over the long run they know I'm going to be honest with them and I am usually not unfair. I allow them to feel, I mean it's O.K. to be happy. It's O.K. to be on top of the world. I think in some ways there's a lot of freedom for them to be whoever they are.

Curriculum and Caring

The children thought many of Martha's lessons and activities were fun—like *bubble-ology*, where the students learned about such physical principles as surface tension by closely observing, experimenting, and just playing with the bubbles they blew. They also really enjoyed making and messing around with *ooblek*, which is a substance that is not a solid, liquid, or a gas but a non-Newtonian fluid, and participating in the *Invention Convention*, where they displayed the inventions they had made for the entire school. Like Noddings (1992), Martha believes that part of caring is providing kids with interesting and challenging things to do. Martha says:

> I want them to be aware of a whole, wide world around them that is there for them to experience and explore. I want them to be confident enough and independent enough in their learning . . . I care that they see learning as something exciting and worthwhile. Something that you do all your life and that it is a good thing to do, a fun thing to do, an interesting thing to do. It enriches your life.

Martha describes her classroom as "nontraditional":

> They sit in groups and can socialize. . . . There are choices for them to make. I think even little things, like being able to go to the bathroom when they want to go . . . a lot of the learning is done through doing. "Doing" kinds of activities, and it is not just a sit-and-listen or sit-and-read or sit-and-write answers but it's

more active . . . we don't go through the textbook from the beginning to the end.

But despite the time and effort Martha expends planning fun and interesting activities for the class, she believes that children's feelings about school depend "not as much on the work that they do but on the relationships with the people in the classroom."

Ways of Caring

She says she doesn't "make a conscious decision to care . . . I don't know that I think about it. I think it's something that is just part of the way I do things. . . . It's just part of the package." Caring, according to Martha, is "treating somebody with respect. I think you can do it without liking somebody." When asked about different ways to show you care for children, Martha explained:

> You notice when someone has a new pair of shoes . . . a button pops off, you sew it back. You take someone home after school or put in extra time after to help somebody do something. . . . Just learning special things for kids. Like trying to find things that you think they are going to be excited about and enjoy. Special things like field trips, parties—not the ordinary stuff—surprises.

There are many highly diverse ways Martha shows children that she cares. The manner in which she helps Sylvia exemplifies a different type of caring. Sylvia is a "bright child who was doing nothing" in school. She had a "terrible attitude problem" and "she wouldn't interact with the other kids because she thought they were beneath her." Martha used a variety of somewhat paradoxical strategies to show she cared for Sylvia:

> I rode her unmercifully. Every time she made some snide nasty remark, I called her on it . . . I lowered her grades dramatically. If she turned in an essay wrong, I gave her an F. And that was her comeuppance—her first F. Sylvia didn't think she could get anything lower than an A. That was sort of the turning point in our relationship, I think, because after that she seemed to think,

"Maybe I'm not as smart as I thought I was. You know there are things for me to learn." . . . Her whole attitude changed. She started developing relationships with the kids in the class. She volunteered to fill in when we needed an extra person in cooperative groups. Her work was fantastic.

WHAT DIFFERENCE DOES A CARING TEACHER MAKE?

As a testimonial to Martha's caring approach, Sylvia, the student described above, wrote Martha the following note as she was about to graduate from fifth grade to middle school:

> It's going to be very hard to leave you! I have had a great time with you. Thanks for all you've done to help me. I'm really going to miss you. You taught me the two most valuable lessons of all: to be myself and to give my all to all I do, to try my hardest, and to do my best. You have been my best teacher and my best friend. You have kept me at the top because you care for me. I want to tell you thanks for everything you've given me, for caring for me, and for being yourself. No one can ever take the place of you.

Other children besides Sylvia also claimed that having a teacher who cares about them made a difference. Many of the children said they like school better, try harder, and make better grades when they know that their teacher cares. Others said they were happier, and it made them "feel better." A few children reported that they were less likely to "get in fights." One child, Candance, said that she was "better able to handle hard times" when she knew her teacher cared about her, because, "if a teacher doesn't care about you, it affects your mind. You feel like you're nobody, and it makes you want to drop out of school."

CONTRADICTIONS IN CARING

Caring is commonly thought of as a positive action designed to assist another. The act of caring, like that of teaching, however, is complex and filled with contradictions. At times even the best intentions of a caring teacher go awry. For example, Martha states firmly that she believes "each child is as deserving of as much energy as any other child." But children have different needs, and some may be more in need than others at certain times. This is one of the great contradictions in caring for children. By choosing to care for one, a teacher has, in essence, chosen not to care for others. Not being able to "meet all those needs all the time is," according to Martha, "the biggest frustration of teaching."

According to these children, a caring teacher is someone who is "there to help you." By *help* most of the children seem to mean that teachers show they care through assisting or guiding them in their school work or by "teaching them." The vast majority of these children believe that a teacher exhibits caring by helping them make sense of their school tasks. The primary role of a caring teacher is to "help you with your work." This seemingly limited view of what characterizes a caring teacher predominates these children's responses. We must ask, then, is children's understanding of formal education and the role of their teachers so limited that they feel not just pleased, but extremely grateful when a teacher personally facilitates their learning?

This response may be interpreted from several perspectives, one of which is that helping is the primary action of teaching; and as such a good teacher, a caring teacher, is one who makes every effort to help children learn. Another, darker, interpretation is that given the realities of public-school teaching with large adult–child ratios and a mandated curriculum, only those teachers who are most concerned about making sure every child learns will actually devote the time and effort needed to help each and every child.

Help is not always enabling; it may even be harmful if it encourages children to depend too heavily upon their teacher or others for assistance. Help may even be damaging; teachers are sometimes directed to teach material they consider worthless. The children's and the teacher's time is wasted when teachers are forced to "help" children learn meaningless facts and skills mandated by the state or school district. The teacher could otherwise spend his or her time helping children learn something meaningful and useful, something they really care about learning.

Another dilemma of caring is also evident in trying to design a curriculum that both excites and engages the children with opportunities to make choices, and the freedom to move around and speak with one another, because an approach that reaches some of the children will not be able to reach others. As Martha points out when asked what she thinks it would have been like to be a student in her classroom this year:

> I think it depends on the kids. For Alisha it was probably great, most of the time. She's sort of a free spirit. For somebody like Brad, it was overwhelming. It was way too much, it was far more than he could handle. I think that more routine for him would have been a lot more secure.

CREATING POSSIBILITIES THROUGH CARING

Caring is, as noted above, a difficult concept to define. It is highly personal and situation specific. There is evidence of something extremely positive going on between Martha and the children. Both the children's remarks and Martha's comments and actions suggest that much of what she does in the classroom with her students is perceived by each of them as caring, and that caring is a part of what is positive about their classroom experience. At the least, the examples below provide some evidence that something good is occurring in this classroom between this fourth-grade teacher and her children.

Robert is a boy who spent last year at a "special" school for children with severe "behavior problems"; during the two previous years he was frequently taken out of class for exhibiting "inappropriate and aggressive" behavior. By November, Robert had become an accepted and productive member of Martha's class and continued to function well the rest of the year. He participated in classroom discussions and activities and appears to have made a few friends.

After failing third grade, Zack entered fourth grade essentially unable to read. By the end of the year, under Martha's guidance and with the help of the Special Education Resource Teacher, Zack was reading at almost a third-grade level.

Martha retained Rhonda and asked to have her in her class again this year. She describes Rhonda as a "bright child, a quick learner, but she doesn't attend very well. It was a challenge to get her to establish more positive relationships with other children." Last year she provoked fights and threw temper tantrums. This year Rhonda has become a well-liked and respected class leader, rather than the manipulative class bully who used and abused relationships with other children to increase her own status and power.

Throughout the fall and into the winter months I observed that while the boys often ate in mixed-race groups, the girls seemed to voluntarily segregate themselves by sitting at separate-by-race tables. In early February, however, I noticed Patricia, a white girl, sitting with a group of African-American girls. From that time on, the girls sat in mixed-race and often mixed-sex grouping for the remainder of the school year. Similarly, two lower income white girls who had been previously excluded from both groups of girls now began sitting with their peers. A number of factors may have influenced this event, including the fact these children were working together on a daily basis in cooperative learning groups. However, Martha's ability to help Patricia and Rhonda work out their differences while they were "science partners" was clearly a crucial factor in encouraging the full integration of these two groups of girls. First, Patricia invited Rhonda to her birthday party; then other mixed-race groups of girls started sitting together at lunch, playing together on the playground, and inviting each other over to their houses and to other birthday parties.

There are many other stories of children whose lives were somehow made a little better because of their positive experiences in Martha Duncan's classroom. Every one of these stories is a different, because Martha influenced each of them in different ways. Not all received an equal "dose" of care. There was at least one child, Brad, who Martha felt she was never able to reach, and several more who certainly did not gain as much from being in her class as others. But no matter who the child was, Martha never gave up trying; she never gave up hope.

What caring for children can do is create enormous possibilities—possibilities like the chance to learn to read, to get excited about learning something new, to feel better about yourself through recognizing your capabilities, and to learn how to work and play with others. Without someone caring, these possibilities are greatly diminished. Without someone caring, it is difficult for children to dream.

REFERENCES

Belenky, M. F., Clinchy, B. M., Goldberger, N. R., & Tarule, J. M. (1986). *Women's ways of knowing: The development of self, voice, and mind.* New York: Basic Books.

Lyons, N. (1983). Two perspectives on self, relationships, and morality. *Harvard Educational Review, 53,* 125–145.

Noddings, N. (1986). Fidelity in teaching, teacher education, and research for teaching. *Harvard Educational Review, 56,* 496-510.

Noddings, N. (1992). *The challenge to care in schools: An alternative approach to education.* New York: Teachers College Press.

Richert, A. E. (1987, April). *Reflection and pedagogical caring: Unsilencing the teacher's voice.* Paper presented at the meeting of the American Educational Research Association, Washington, DC.

Ward, J. (1990, October). Presentation at the Lilly Endowment Grants Program on Youth Caring, Indianapolis.

Part II

Schools: Multiple Manifestations of Caring

Chapter 3

Contradictions and Conflicts in Caring

Susan T. Danin

Nel Noddings (1984) talks about caring as existing in the relationship between two people, the one-caring and the one-cared-for. The fundamental aspect of a caring relationship, according to Noddings, is the ability of the one caring to "apprehend the reality" of the one cared for. Caring in this context means to understand and accept what the other is experiencing in any given circumstance: that is from that person's point of view. *Natural* or *authentic caring* is subjective, nonrational, receptive, and responsive. Gilligan (1984), in her studies of moral development, found females more likely than males to engage in authentic caring or to practice an "ethic of caring." In education, traditionally, the one-caring is the teacher and the student is the one-cared-for.

Noddings also describes *aesthetic caring* as caring about ideas and things. Aesthetic caring is objective, rational, and abstract. Males tend to practice what Gilligan (1984) identified as an "ethic of justice." Evidence of aesthetic caring abounds in education. It exists whenever groups of people make decisions about other groups of people, as in, for example, the development of standardized curricula or various systems of teacher and student evaluation (Apple, 1984; McNeil, 1988a, b). The interaction between the apparent contradictions in caring causes very real conflicts for teachers, administrators, students, and families.

In the following chapter I describe a situation in which multiple opportunities existed for caring and being cared for among teachers, administrators, and students. However, what emerged was a basic "contradiction in caring" that gave rise to multiple conflicts.

The focus of this study was the members of a team, formed as part of a project, to help students at risk for school failure. The project, from its inception, revealed a basic contradiction between the ethic of caring that existed among the teachers in the elementary school in which this study took place, and caring as defined by the project. The contradiction existed between subjective, nonrational (authentic) caring and objective, rational (aesthetic) caring. The conflicts that arose out of this basic contradiction had serious impacts on both the members of the team and the school at large.

The data for this study were collected during the first year of the project, while the author participated as a member of the team. The data consist of transcripts of audiorecordings of committee meetings, interviews with the staff, school documents, and observations of classrooms and faculty meetings. Using standard ethnographic techniques, the impact of the project was revealed through the words and actions of the participants.

THE PROJECT

A local business foundation approached the superintendent of City School System with an offer to fund a program at the high school to improve race relations in the community. The superintendent had been concerned about the discrepancy in achievement scores between white and black students, along with other evidence that black students were not experiencing the same level of success in school as white students. She envisioned a project that would generate programs for at risk (predominantly black) students that could lead to their academic success as well as improve race relations. Believing that intervention must begin with children's earliest school experience, she wanted to provide funds to an elementary school. The foundation readily agreed to fund the project, and an elementary school was selected as the pilot with the goal of developing a "replicable model" for working with at-risk students. The emphasis from the project was clearly to show results—that is, to increase achievement test scores, to increase friendships among black and white children, and to increase the involvement of black parents in school. To make sure the project had some guidance in the best practices and evaluation, a liaison from a nearby university was hired to work closely with the school.

THE SCHOOL

To better understand the context in which the project took place, it is important to look briefly at the school's beginnings. Landville Elementary School was established in the fall of 1970 as the only "open education" school in the system. Desegregation had occurred three years previously, but discipline problems, arguments over what to teach, and a lack of trust from the community continued to plague the system. Landville was, according to the principal who had been with the school since 1973, set up to "get positive involvement for the teachers and students" and to "be a good place for kids."

The school was built in a wooded area on the outskirts of the town and originally comprised an administration building and three open classroom areas called *pods*. It was modeled on the British Infant Schools, and the faculty who had requested to work there were described as "dedicated" and "committed." The curriculum was designed to allow optimum interaction between students and teachers. Together, teachers and students created handcrafts, such as quilts and soap, and had sleepovers and campouts. Teachers were allowed to bring their own young children to school with them.

Three years into the program, the district pressured the school to reemphasize academic skills, because the students' achievement test scores were falling below the national average. The principal recalled that the major challenge was, "Could we show we could do as well academically and still have a good atmosphere?'' Over the next three years the staff "worked weekends and nights" to build more structure into open education. Achievement scores rose to above the national mean, where they have remained ever since. This continued to be a point of pride for the principal who felt they successfully met the challenge.

Over the past 20 years the school has grown from the charter faculty of 10 teachers to a total staff of 21 classroom teachers, four special education teachers, four special services teachers (art, dance, music, P.E.) and 15 full-time aides. The facility has expanded to include a kindergarten/first grade pod and eight mobile units. At the time of the study there were 532 students in kindergarten through sixth grade. The racial composition of the student body was 75% white, 19% black, and 6% Hispanic.

THE TEAM

The principal decided to form a team of teachers for the purpose of planning during the first year of what they were told would be a three to four year project. The team participants were specially handpicked by the principal for their experience and commitment to the "education of all children." The team consisted of six classroom teachers, one representing each grade level, a special education teacher, a counselor, the family specialist, the vice-principal, the principal, and the university liaison. Three of the teachers had been with the school since it opened, and all the team's members had been in education for over ten years. Four members were black, eight were white, and all but one were women. The team met a total of 13 times over the school year to discuss and plan for the project.

THE CONTRADICTIONS

The teachers at Landville had an ethic of caring that was extremely personal, interactive, and time intensive. Teachers focused on "success" for their students for quite some time, but the project, with its funding and emphasis on measurable outcomes for a specific group of children, required that teachers make their previous forms of caring conform to a new model of caring. Figure 3.1 summarizes some of the major areas of conflict that existed between the type of caring practiced by teachers and the caring practiced by administrators.

Aesthetic Caring (Project)	Authentic Caring (Teachers)
Rational/Objective Caring	Nonrational/Subjective Caring
Originates in a group outside the school (Central Office; Univ)	Originates between teacher and student inside classrooms
Global/idealistic goals	Day-to-day realistic goals
Narrow black-and-white achievement gap	Get students to bring material to class
Improve race relations	Get students to bring in homework
Decisions are rule bound	Decisions are circumstance bound
Systematic evaluation	Intuition/faith

Figure 3.1   Contradictions in Caring

The conflicts that inevitably arose from these inherent contradictions were played out over the year during the team meetings. Efforts to resolve these conflicts had multiple, usually unintended, consequences. Team members expressed frustration and resentment and spoke of feeling overwhelmed and helpless. They were caught between their ethic of caring for children in highly personal ways and the need both to provide school-wide interventions and to prove that something good was happening for at-risk students for the project.

CONFLICTS

The person who experienced the most conflict was the principal. Her conflict largely resided in the basic contradiction in caring between the project and the teachers She embodied what Noddings (1984) has described as trying to integrate the "feminine" approach" with a traditionally "masculine approach" into a workable ethic in education. The conflict was most apparent between her "feminine" role as one-caring and her "masculine" role as administrator guided by the dictates of logic and justice. She worked to reconcile her personal/female caring for the teachers with her institutional/male caring for the school. Her caring was divided among several cared-for persons— teachers, students, and parents—which created endless multiple dilemmas for her. The conflict and the guilt it engendered were thus part of her daily reality.

The typical expression of this conflict was her mixed communication to the teachers. She told the team members, "It's [the project] got to be in a way that we're not going . . . to completely change the role of the teacher to someone who is almost a martyr to the cause. That's not going to happen. Teachers are not to make sacrifices to the cause." She well understood that teachers had full schedules during school and busy lives outside school. However, her own behavior sent another message. She stayed at school often into the evening, came in on weekends, and was always accessible to her faculty. She was reported to "really listen and see the strengths in everyone." She singled out teachers who were doing extra things with students as exemplars. She took a child to the beach one weekend and recounted to team members later how happy she was when this same child "came up and hugged me in the cafeteria." Every day she modeled the ethic of caring that had always been associated with Landville.

The project also created much tension in the relationship between the principal and the teachers. The teachers felt that the principal had agreed to participate in something that put undue pressure on them to perform publicly and show successful results. The principal, in turn, cited outside experts to show the teachers how rational what they were being asked to do was: "One of the things that the research says is that children need to feel that the teachers are warm and supportive of them, and we're trying to be more warm and supportive." The principal wanted the school to look good. She took great pride in being the principal of this innovative school and often bragged about how the faculty had attended many workshops over the years to improve curriculum and teaching practices. Landville had an excellent reputation for working closely with the university and for implementing research-based programs for improving education for all children. However, one outside observer commented, "There hasn't been a steady state [at the school] for quite a while. It hasn't been, 'Okay, we've got our act in gear, let's roll with it for awhile.' Its always something or another."

The principal worried about the teachers and how they felt about what was happening. When she heard criticism about how she was not listening to what the teachers needed, she scheduled one whole committee meeting to work with two teachers. "We just need to talk and understand what [this teacher] has in mind, Why don't we just get together" Her care for the school (impersonal and fair) conflicted with her care for the well-being of the teachers (personal and subjective).

The team itself was divided. The ethic of caring was not acceptable for the project (the superintendent, the foundation, or the university) because it was not objective, quantifiable, and replicable. The words used when discussing the project, *goals, strategies, objectives, replicable model,* and *evaluation,* were antithetical to the teachers way of caring. Caring meant knowing and working with an individual child and his or her family, so the child felt good about school. The conflict coalesced the members into three general roles: the resisters, the idealists, and the realists, with various team members finding themselves playing different roles at different times.

Resisters did not want to change their relationships with students. They were already doing the right thing. They talked about not having time to "sit around and think things up" (because they were already "busy" caring). They considered the project "a waste of time." The planning meetings, release time from class, and time spent filling out forms kept them "apart in human affairs" (Noddings, 1984). They were trying to care for their ethical selves by holding onto their own ethic of care. It was not, however, an accident that they were members of the team. The principal had picked them because they represented the school and the principal's ethic of caring. They argued, complained, or withdrew during the meetings. In response to filling out a checklist of student behaviors, one teacher declared, "But my kids would look so bad on paper! That's why I can't do it, so I don't want to be told I have to, okay? I don't want to!"

Idealists acted out the project's model of aesthetic caring. They were prepared to move from personal caring to caring about ideas and things in the abstract. One idealist stated, "If we are in the business of education, we hope that one day, with our support, they [the at-risk students] will get there on their own steam." They worked to generate a definition for identifying children and methods to document change. They designed a checklist of needs and discussed categorizing the children in "tiers," from those who were most to those least in need of help. The idealists adopted the language of the administrators and researchers.

Realists functioned as mediators. They became the ones-caring by reducing the tension, guilt, and frustration the others were feeling. They were "apprehending the reality" of their fellow teachers: "We can't be all things to all people" . . . "What we do as part of the project is our decision" . . . "I think we need to know it's okay. We're just going to do what we do, and that's it. It's fine." They constantly negotiated between the resisters and idealists.

Conflict arose when the team tried to define their task. The nature of the project required that the team members engage in aesthetic caring. The team, as a group, was asked to make decisions about a group of students labeled at-risk. The Idealists on the team saw their task was to identify students according to some objective definition, to generate broad based interventions, and to evaluate student progress. Resisters wanted to continue as before, to help any child *they* felt needed help, not because of a label given to a student or a cut-off score on a test. They wanted to know that they still had a choice to help a student if a student did not "fit" the definition of *at-risk*

The biggest conflict emerged over the teachers' obligation to prove that something was actually happening with the at-risk students as a result of the different interventions. The whole issue of accountability to an outside agency caused particular resentment in the teachers. At the meeting, when the vice-principal announced that they would be required to write a quarterly report to the foundation to communicate what the teachers had been doing, the team's reaction was swift and strong. They wanted to make sure that the foundation would not be able to dictate to them how they should proceed as professionals. One teacher declared, "I'll tell you what, at this point, if they cut it [the money] for the project off, it would be a damn blessing in my opinion!" Another reminded the team that they had not seen any money yet, implying that the foundation did not, in fact, have the right to ask them for anything. Someone else commented, "The thing is that we're all trying [someone interjected, "Right"], we're all doing things all the time." Another teacher added, "We'll probably have to document, you know, and I'll probably have to document every time I talk to a kid!" It was clear during this meeting that the teachers resented the intrusion on their time and the requirement to respond to the evaluation demands placed on them by the project.

Teachers told individual stories about their caring relationships with students. They measured success or failure with their at-risk students according to how they felt about these relationships. One teacher stated, "Isn't it amazing? . . . We do the right things and nobody believes it!" They spoke of different ways with different children and making decisions intuitively about what worked to nurture relationships with each child. One teacher, who consistently practiced an ethic of caring, recounted, "I just looked at [a student] and said something like 'I'm going to be really upset if you do that' [laughing]. What else was I going [to do]." She continued, "Well, I did say that to [another student] and he did care, but you see, I don't have the relationship with [this student]." This left the teachers vulnerable to conflict in other ways.

The idea of reciprocity in the caring relationship means that the one cared for must be willing to receive the caring. When this is absent, so is caring (Noddings, 1984). "Success" occurred when the teacher cared for a student and the student, in turn, received the teacher's caring—for example, the principal's hug in the cafeteria. The vice-principal recounted an experience he had with a student who was always in trouble: "Since I was always seeing him as a disciplinarian, now I see him constantly as a buddy; he stops, comes in, chats with me . . . Every day he stops." "Failure" could result when the student's reality went against what the teacher felt was right or best and the teacher no longer responded to the student, or when the student failed to receive the care that was extended. It was common for teachers to take team meeting time to share personal stories of children. They all listened and tried to help each other. One teacher's story of a particularly difficult child caused her great distress and took up almost one whole meeting. When the caring relationship was incomplete, teachers either overtly withdrew or they maintained the mere appearance of caring. Noddings (1984) cautions against confusing caring for the subject—that is, for feeling craft pride—with caring for the student himself or herself. The central office administrators' emphasis on evaluation constantly reminded the teachers that academic achievement was the valued goal. If teachers are pressured to devalue caring for the student first, authentic caring cannot be present.

Because of the personal/interactive nature of their caring, teachers wondered where they would find the time: "I simply have too many at-risk students in my class to help them!" This was a teacher who had always spent extra time working with students and contacting parents. She was reacting to the model of caring dictated by the project, not her own ethic of caring. Teachers had to fill out forms documenting what they were doing (supplemental activities, contacts with parents), and turn them in on a periodic basis. It was the time for record keeping that could never be found, not the time to spend with a student. This became obvious when an administrator offered substitute teachers to release time for record keeping, and the teachers expressed grave concern over missing valuable time with the same children about whom they were meeting! The resisters rejected the offer of substitute teachers. The idealists took a half-day release time to work on the definition, but took advantage of the opportunity only once during the entire year.

Demands from other students and professional growth workshops, as well as the new demands from the project, structured the day so that it was virtually impossible to "care" for their students in ways teachers valued. This caused such a rift in the faculty morale that some people stated openly, "We can't make people who don't choose to do these things feel guilty!"

THE IMPACT: CARING AT RISK

Conflict and guilt are the inevitable risks and costs of caring (Noddings, 1984). Authentic caring means total involvement in the one-cared-for. It was no wonder that these teachers felt completely overwhelmed when they found themselves dividing their caring among several children, the principal, and each other. A university supervisor who had worked with the faculty for several years observed that, as a result of their involvement with the project, "They really have been asked to feel guilty on a lot of different levels about what they're doing or not doing."

The team members spent several meetings discussing who the at-risk students were. The idea of being confined by a definition but needing to document strategies and change put the teachers in a dilemma. They wanted the freedom to work with whomever they felt needed help, but they did not want to have to "waste" time filling out forms on everyone they helped. They talked about feeling "overwhelmed" and "inadequate," and spoke in angry tones to each other.

The conflict between the principal and the team members caused guilt on the teachers' part, because they liked and respected her. One teacher described the principal as an administrator who "understands us individually . . . her attitude of understanding every one individually, our strengths, the things we do well and want to do, so she encourages that all the time and since she's always encouraging that, then we aren't afraid to be whoever we are in whatever area you're going to go." The blend of pronouns (we, our, you) in this quote was particularly revealing of the caring way this teacher felt about her peers, as well as the principal herself.

The principal, for her part, wanted to create an atmosphere of "freedom for people to try their hunches." She strongly resisted the idea of ranking the activities by priority or giving any one part of the program more weight than the others. The teachers knew, however, that they were expected to keep anecdotal records, complete behavior checklists, and to try new instructional techniques. They were caught between freedom and obligation, and, therefore, felt overwhelmed, inadequate, and guilty. Guilt made caring obligatory. Throughout the year, compromises were made based on what teachers believed the principal wanted. Their caring became a burden.

Much of the team's energy was also spent trying to figure out how to involve the rest of the faculty who continually expressed frustration about decisions made without input from them. One teacher said that people felt like "decisions are coming from God" (referring to the team). "There is such hostility going on . . . there's no togetherness." Another pinpointed the project itself as the culprit, "I just feel so tense that I just want to walk out and say, 'Don't give me any money; I don't want to do anything with it. Leave me alone!'"

The cumulative effect of feeling helpless, inadequate, and guilty resulted in teachers' resistance to doing anything connected with the project. The structure and systematization the project imposed created such conflicts for teachers that it was literally killing the desire to help at-risk children!

Documentation, evaluation, and measurement all served to objectify persons. The teachers as well as the students were being turned into study objects. Noddings describes it as "when groups of individuals discuss the perceived needs of another individual or group, the imperative changes from 'I must do something' to 'something must be done.' This change is accompanied by a shift from the non-rational and subjective to the rational and objective. Authentic caring gets transformed into problem-solving. Caring becomes focused in the requirement and disappears; only the illusion (of caring) remains" (1984, p. 25). The project was the arena in which the implicit contradictions in caring became explicit.

When multiple "pulls" to care exist, people tend to rely on rules and customary standards of behavior. At Landville, the standard of behavior had been to give more individual time, which, in this situation, just increased the burden and guilt. The irony was that the teachers risked losing their ethic of caring for others, in order to care for their own ethical selves. They generated "rule-bound responses in the name of caring" (Noddings, 1984, p. 24). The developed a working definition, documentation forms, and started a buddy "system" that paired a teacher with an at-risk student. While these rules may have serval to protect, they also alienated teachers from authentic caring relationships.

By mid-year, the climate in school had become so negative, the team pulled together in order to "take care" of each other. Two full faculty meetings were held to create an arena for creative dialogue. The principal renamed the team the *effective school committee*, which she claimed would reconnect it to the whole school's plan. The tone of the team meetings shifted, someone said, "We need to help kids first." Another concurred, "We are spending too much time mumbling about being jerked around [by the project] and need to start spending more time on helping the kids." They tried to return to their ethic of caring, the relationships built between teachers and students and teachers to each other.

By the end of the first year, the team had basically disbanded. From the original 12 members, a core of five remained, only two of whom were teachers. Additionally, fewer and fewer meetings were held. From the point of view of the teachers, the project was something that would remain external to their ethic of caring.

CONCLUSION

It is evident from the above narrative that the school's participation in the project engendered much contradiction, conflict, and guilt. On first inspection, what appeared to evolve was the illusion of aesthetic caring. However, the project existed in name only. Teachers complied minimally with completing forms. Quarterly reports were faithfully sent to the foundation and the superintendent, but they were written by two team members with no involvement from the others. A co-director of the after-school tutorial program for at-risk students promised to do the paperwork in order to "make the program look good." It looked like teachers were conducting "business as usual."

However, something had changed. The teachers at Landville never openly dealt with the conflict and guilt engendered by their participation in the project. They engaged in resistance and minimal compliance and, in the end, effectively diffused its influence on their daily lives, but there was a "cost" to this kind of resolution. At the heart of caring is the "apprehension of the other's reality." Because the teachers were not apprehending their own reality, they continued to feel conflict and guilt. Evidence of this was found in their residual anger and resentment of anything that represented the project (for example, the superintendent or the foundation). Another vital conflict between the teachers and the principal was not resolved. Contradiction was inherent in the principal's role, and because she and the teachers practiced an ethic of caring, they continually experienced conflict and guilt. The project exacerbated the principal's conflicts and, as a result, the conflict between her and the teachers. The question became, could the teachers or the principal continue to engage in authentic caring while using energy to deny their own reality?

Noddings (1984) talks of "acts of courage" in the experience of guilt: to recognize and accept guilt as the natural part of caring. One might even question the genuineness of caring if conflict and guilt were never experienced. Authentic and aesthetic caring are not mutually exclusive. The challenge becomes how to create an environment within which the nonrational and subjective can cohabitate with the rational and objective, particularly when the tradition has been to favor the rational and devalue the other. Theorists (Gilligan & Phelps, 1988; Noddings, 1984) have argued this devaluing is because an ethic of caring is associated with women and women's work. Because of this tradition of devaluing an ethic of caring, Noddings claims we must nurture an ethic of caring, and that teachers need to "nurture their own ethical ideals" within the larger system.

The first step is for the participants in a caring relationship to engage in a dialogue, which means maintaining an openness to discuss whatever anyone wants to discuss. This takes time and the willingness to listen, share, and respond. The faculty of Landville made a good beginning, but the lack of time was always an issue. The practice of caring means sharing and negotiating actions in genuine partnership. Noddings states, "we need to accept their (teachers, principals, and students) reality and find out what they are doing and work with them about mutual goals, sharing experiences" (1984, p. 196). When this occurs, then the ones-caring and the ones-cared-for are confirmed, and an authentic caring relationship is completed.

How the staff of Landville accepted and resolved the contradictions and conflicts of caring has continued to unfold. At the end of the first year they were not engaged in dialogue. There was evidence that teachers were withdrawing to care for their own ethical selves (Noddings, 1984). Three teachers announced that they would tutor their own students next year rather than send them to a schoolwide tutoring program. Another teacher stated she would do "nothing extra." Many remarked that morale was low. There was a sense of loss of the "community" that had historically flourished in Landville.

Perhaps, then, this has been the ultimate "expense" of devaluing an ethic of caring. Landville's story is not unusual in education. There are always too many students, too little time, and demands that are not of the teachers' or students' choosing. What is particularly poignant is that Landville is a school whose beginnings valued and nurtured an ethic of caring, yet three years after it opened, the principal and teachers had felt the pressure to shift the value to aesthetic caring. The team's response to the project was a reflection of the continuing struggle in the contradiction: their ethic of caring itself is "at risk!"

We may ask, "Can the aims of aesthetic caring and authentic caring work together? Does one always occur at the expense of the other?" The answer remains to be found in the experiences of people in schools.

REFERENCES

Apple, M. W. (1984). Teaching and women's work: A comparative historical and ideological analysis. In E. B. Gumbert (Ed.), *Expressions of power in education* (Vol. 3, pp.29–49). Atlanta: Georgia State University, Center for Cross-cultural Education.

Gilligan, C. (1984). *In a different voice.* Cambridge, MA: Harvard University Press.

Gilligan, C., & Phelps, E.B. (1988, August). *Seeking connection: New insights and questions for teachers.* Presented at the Center for the Study of Gender,

Education and Human Development, Harvard Graduate School of Education. Cambridge, MA.

McNeil, L. M. (1988a). Contradictions of control, Part 1: Administrators and teachers. *Phi Delta Kappan, 69,* 333–339.

McNeil, L. M. (1988b). Contradictions of control, Part 3: Contradictions of reform. *Phi Delta Kappan, 69,* 478–485.

Noddings, N. (1984). *Caring: A feminine approach to ethics and moral education.* Berkeley, CA: University of California Press.

Chapter 4

The Prinicipal as Caregiver*

Michael Courtney
George W. Noblit

The literature on caring tends to emphasize personal interactions as the prime locus of caring (Gilligan, 1982, 1988; Noddings, 1984). This emphasis is understandable in that caring is an alternative to the all-too-instrumental perspectives that characterize educational thought and practice. The caring perspective refocuses us on the relationships between people as the key element in education and causes us, appropriately, to doubt the effectiveness and significance of "systems" that seek to organize practice, train educators, and govern schools. In this sense, caring is more than a corrective for the many years of misguided thinking about education. Indeed, it is a fundamental challenge to how we conceive of education and its improvement. Complaints about the caring perspective from policymakers and other people who propose a "remote control of teaching" (Shulman, 1983) should come as no surprise. The caring perspective dismisses this possibility and thus threatens the power they wish to yield. If the relationship between teachers and students is the critical element in education, then there is little logic in attempts to reform the "systems" of education that are at best peripheral to the teacher–student relationship or, worse,

*This work was supported by a grant from the Lilly Endowment Program on Youth and Caring.

67

construct barriers to caring. The chapter by Susan Danin in this volume shows this in graphic detail.

Yet Noddings (1984) argues that there is a type of caring that is outside interpersonal relationships. The distinction she draws is between *authentic* and *aesthetic* caring. The former is found in reciprocal relationships of care, the latter in a more abstract commitment to ideas, to practices or contexts beyond the interpersonal level. Put in this way, aesthetic caring can be viewed as not "real" caring, but as some approximation thereof. We agree that this distinction is important. However, we wish to argue that it may be a mistake to assume that social roles or formal positions that place people outside the essential *authentic caring* in the teacher–student relationship are only about *aesthetic* caring. Our educational "systems" are, after all, sets of relationships as well as rules and regulations. Obviously, caring can emerge in any of the relationships present in our educational institutions, although, also obviously, it may not. It even may be chagrined as favoritism or other supposed threats to the impartiality so valued in bureaucracies. The relationships that do not involve the students directly, but are concerned with the students, may be best seen as hybrid forms of aesthetic and authentic caring.

Our argument is that while the key caring relationship in education is between teacher and student, other relationships are also important and about caring, even if quite unlike that between teacher and student. We do not wish to overemphasize this or argue for the necessity of these other relationships, for, indeed, these relationships may not be necessary. Our argument is more pragmatic. These other relationships exist and, if history is any predictor of the future, are likely to for some time. Given this, we think it is worthwhile to consider how these relationships ought to be constituted, how we ought to mix "authentic" and "aesthetic" caring. Although our intent may be normative, we also do not wish to argue that we have these answers. We do not. We think answers can only come from detailed examinations of many specific cases of caring. Our intent is simply to start this process by examining one case: the case of a principal who tried to care and tried to bring caring into the language and culture of one school.

We think this case requires an expansive definition of *caring*, such as that offered by Fisher and Tronto (1990, p.40). They argue that caring should be viewed as "a species activity that includes everything we do to maintain, continue, and repair our world so that we can live in it as well as possible." They also argue that caring can be conceived of as a process of overlapping and intertwining phases of "caring about, taking care of, caregiving and care-receiving" (p. 40). They argue that each is a "general precondition for the next" (p. 40) but may be "intertwined in chaotic and contradictory styles" (p. 41). Further, they see caring also as a practice that requires the people involved to have certain preconditional "ability factors" such as "time, material resources, knowledge and skill" (p. 41). We will use Fisher and Tronto's conceptualization as a way of organizing the case we present here. It helps us reconceptualize a case we know very personally. Michael lived it; George watched and tried to help.

THE SCHOOL

George Watts Elementary School is the oldest school in Durham, North Carolina. It was built in 1916 on the edge of the central business district to serve a white, upper middle-class neighborhood. Over the years the attendance zones have been redrawn many times both by the district and by the courts as part of school desegregation. Presently, two distinct neighborhoods are represented in Watts School. One is the traditional neighborhood of white, upper-middle-class Trinity Park residents. The other is the working class, African-American neighborhood of Walltown. The school serves 300 students in kindergarten through fifth grades, 65% of whom are African-American. The classrooms average about 24 students each in size. Thirty women serve these children as teachers and teacher assistants (the latter being concentrated in kindergarten through third grades). The principals at Watts, throughout its long history, were generally authoritarian and endorsed rather traditional approaches to instruction. This was true regardless of the gender of the principal. Watts School only had two males principals, each for relatively short periods of time, prior to Michael's arrival in the fall of 1987.

The years before Michael's arrival had been turbulent ones. Since desegregation in 1973, there had existed a tension between the Trinity Park and Walltown communities, in part due to the closing of Walltown school and the transfer of Walltown students to desegregate Watts School. Trinity Park traditionally viewed the school as theirs, even as the demography shifted to majority African-American students and teachers. They controlled the Parents Teachers Association and had become overly intrusive, according to the faculty, in the daily life of the classrooms. Walltown resented the closing of its school, even at this late date, and felt belittled in the presence of Trinity Park parents. By the mid-1980s, the turmoil had reached a peak. Watts School had three principals in three years. Each left for different reasons, but the school had been wracked by the changes—even though the school's various constituencies had directly engineered the principal transitions. The superintendent had polled the school's constituencies, who indicated they wanted a caring principal to bring unity and stability to the school. Michael was hired with this mandate.

Michael was faced with a dilemma. In a school that had had so many principals who had operated in so many different ways, he could not just continue recent policies. These were seen as failures. Moreover, he could not initiate a host of new policies and procedures that could cause more turmoil. He brought his dilemma to George, whom he knew through graduate coursework. Their discussion led to two initiatives. First was a school–university partnership, and second was a democratic approach to leadership. The first meant that George and some graduate students would be working on writing a history of the school. This meant ongoing interviews with the teachers—our source of data on teacher beliefs and perceptions that we will report in this chapter. It also meant that George would be able to observe Michael's work over the next few years and serve as a confidant. The second meant that Michael went to the teachers to help define what ought to be done. This meant that teachers came to define Michael as "caring about" them, the children and the school.

CARING ABOUT

Fisher and Tronto (1990) see the first phase in caring to be *caring about*. By this they mean a process of selecting and attending to things that affect survival and well-being. It presumes a connection with others and an orientation that focuses on "continuity, maintenance and repair" (p. 40). While we clearly did not have Fisher and Tronto's work to guide us at the time, Michael was involved early in trying to develop his ability to care about the school and its many and diverse participants.

Developing connections with people is always difficult, but more so when one has an official position and responsibility. Such a position communicates to others that at some point you may have to act in accordance with your responsibility to the possible detriment of other commitments and connections. In this way, an official position may undermine caring. The parents and teachers at Watts recognized this and were wary, even though they welcomed Michael and the promise of stability that his appointment symbolized to the school. It was clearly Michael's burden to first demonstrate he cared about the school before the teachers would invest their energies in him or in projects he sponsored.

His first task was to develop connections with the faculty and parents. He began immediately to introduce himself to the faculty and to parents who came to the school. He worked to be visible in the school and community, and to take time to talk and visit with everyone he could. Over time these encounters led to significant bonds being developed. However, these encounters and connections were based on opportunity—meaning that many people that he wished to reach were left unattended. These encounters were also individual, while his official mandate was a corporate one: to bring stability and unity to the school. In many ways, this was one of the first clashes of aesthetic and authentic caring. He had to care about both the individuals he had committed to lead and the institutional entity everyone termed *the school*. This term has important symbolic content. Most significantly, it had two often contradictory meanings. *The school* was a symbol of a shared destiny of the faculty and students and, to a lesser extent, the parents. It was also a symbol of Trinity Park—a white enclave in an increasingly minority city. Michael's attempt to care about the corporate identity, the school, was made problematic by these contradictory meanings. His challenge was to reconstitute the symbolic meaning in the long run, while trying to emphasize the meaning that implied a shared destiny of teachers and students.

There were no established mechanisms for Michael to demonstrate his caring about the school except through the traditional faculty and PTA meetings. These he continued, but tried to provide for more substantive agendas and wider participation. Clearly, this is aesthetic caring: symbols are celebrated symbolically and rituals have ritualized meanings. The commitment was to these more abstract elements of school culture and less embedded in the interpersonal relationships that make authentic caring possible. They did help to indicate his commitment to democratic participation and decision making, but did little to develop the relationships that would make his caring about the school more profound. Michael created mechanisms that enabled him to develop relationships with subsets of people. He created two advisory boards. The internal advisory council was constituted with a teacher representative from each grade level, and was a forum to discuss issues and policies, and to formulate questions to bring to the full faculty and/or PTA. This enabled him to establish a connection with people from each grade level and to try to communicate his caring about the school and to get input about how to demonstrate this.

The external advisory board was designed to develop connections with a broader range of constituents and to try to get them to care about the school in clearly aesthetic ways, involving material resources, political support, and knowledge. This board was composed of one internal advisory council member, parent representatives (from both Trinity Park and Walltown), professors from nearby universities, government and church representatives, and even a member of the local school board.

These mechanisms provided a forum for relationships to begin and established Michael's commitment to the school. He also initiated the oral history project with George and graduate students from a nearby university. The project was conceived as a way to capture the history of the school (purposively defined as including the history of Walltown School also). This history was to give people an opportunity to talk about their individual and collective rememberances, to do something that the communities might find interesting, and as a way to discover how the symbolic content of the "the school" might be reconstituted. In other words, it was a community service project that afforded Michael more time to learn about the culture of the school and establish a different type of connection. An unanticipated consequence of the children and the university researchers interviewing people about the school was people coming to believe that the school was caring more about them.

Michael also had to live up to his responsibility to evaluate teachers, a process that in many ways can be most traumatic to teacher–principal relationships. Yet Michael tried to frame this responsibility in ways that showed he cared about the school. He engaged initially in close supervision of instruction but coupled it with an emphasis on coaching the teacher to improved evaluations. He asked teachers to set their own goals for improvement, tried to provide appropriate professional development opportunites, and evaluated their progress both formatively and summatively. Few people actually enjoy being evaluated, especially when the evaluator takes his job seriously. However, Michael was able to communicate that he cared about the school and his teachers, would work with them to resolve issues, and expected quality classroom instruction. He also demonstrated that he was interested in the relationships the teachers were developing with their students as well as the content and technical adequacy of their instruction. Caring about, for Michael, was coupled with improvement—caring enough to try to do better.

TAKING CARE OF

The real activity of any school is consumed with the second phase of *caring*, the activities of *taking care of*. The day-to-day life in schools revolves around taking care of students and others. Fisher and Tronto (1990) argue that *caring about* "does not necessarily involve any overt action" (p. 42). *Taking care of* implies action, even if it is short of actual caregiving. In this phase, caring is actualized as a moral commitment. It also means that caring is going public, that others are involved and can hold you accountable for your actions and can choose to reciprocate or not. Fisher and Tronto argue that *taking care of* involves judgments and resources. One has to judge the relative worth of various actions and judge what resources they will require to fulfill the moral commitment to take care of.

While teachers have a rather clear responsibility to take care of children in their classrooms, the moral responsibility of the principal is more diffuse. Michael clearly defined his role as taking care of the teachers, even though his contact with them individually or collectively was limited. However, as caring is relational, he also had to discover what the teachers interpreted as being taken care of. In casual conversations, Michael was supportive and respectful, and tried to respond to expressed needs and wishes. In the usual arenas for collective meetings (committee meetings, internal advisory council meetings, faculty meetings), he tried to solicit direction from the teachers. His early focus on stability and unity gave way to a teacher-driven request for a stronger discipline policy. Here his concern for the children tempered his concern for taking care of the teachers. He developed a schoolwide discipline system, based loosely on ideas of assertive discipline (Canter & Canter, 1976), that also allowed teachers to decide what was especially important to their own classrooms. He diverted pressures for a more punitive discipline code by inviting teacher participation in a study of caring in classrooms that George and the university personnel were interested in doing. This meant that he could try to focus on a more proactive approach rather than a more punitive one. It also meant that the teachers would have a strong role in defining what was important in their classrooms. Indeed, Michael noted that discipline infractions declined during the year of the caring classroom ethnographies and intensive interviews with teachers, even though that had not been an intent of the project or the discipline code.

The oral history project enabled him to learn another way teachers define being taken care of. When he was initially discussing the project with the teachers at a faculty meeting, they thought it was a fine idea but not of much relevance to their work. They asked, "What will it do for the children?" We learned that one of the things teachers used to make judgements about whether initiatives were significant to them was if they did something that had an impact on their essential responsibility to take care of the children. Our response was to redesign the project to include some of the fourth- and fifth-grade students, teaching them how to interview and having them conduct some of the interviews. The teachers thought this made the project much more salient and began to actively support it. Our working with the "Junior Tarheel Historians" and other fourth- and fifth-grade students to develop an interview guide that the students thought was interesting to them (but not necessarily to the adults) led to a teacher leaving the room commenting positively that "they'll do fine." The project became an acceptable way to take care of the teachers by "doing something good for the children." Teachers also were intensively interviewed by George and a team of graduate students about their life histories and the history of both schools. Both the content of the interviews, and being interviewed itself, came to be interpreted as evidence that the principal and researchers did care about the views of the teachers. As the project developed and community interest in the school increased, the teachers also came to interpret the project as taking care of them by enhancing their image in the community and developing a sense of continuity to their lives and work (Noddings, 1992).

Michael also tried to "take care of" the teachers by promoting professional development. Instead of starting initiatives to change the school and the teachers' practice, he began by having the teachers set school goals and then structured staff development to help people be more effective at what they wished to accomplish. This demonstrated a respect for the teachers' capabilities while also supporting improvement. The improvement was accomplished through inservice training in cooperative learning, hands-on science methods, whole language, oral history and social studies, student retention, and student memory. It is also evident that public schools are limited in providing incentives for teachers and Watts School was no different. The teachers were supportive of improvement efforts for their own reasons, but this was bolstered by Michael trying to show appreciation through conversations, written notes, staff luncheons, and featuring teachers in special articles in the local media and in professional publications. He reestablished rituals that had been long lost but were recovered by the oral history project. The school song was sung often, and a mascot was chosen who later appeared in costume at school events. Community assemblies were held quarterly where students would talk to the entire school about their accomplishments and plans. Award certificates were given for all grades. These ritual and symbolic affairs clearly did not directly end up in teachers giving care, rather they were celebratory markers that the school was being taken care of.

Michael also judged it important that he take care of the communities that Watts School served. The Trinity Park families were clear that the school was essential to their identity as a neighborhood. This was in part because the school had served their children for over 75 years and in part because a teacher and the school were embodied in a novel that these families interpreted to be about them. The novel was a powerful narrative, recounted repeatedly in our interviews with people for the oral history project. While students from Trinity Park were a decided minority in the school, their parents controlled the PTA and were ever vigilant about the school's reputation. As Fisher and Tronto argue, caring is full of contradictions and conflicts, and this was not the least.

The Walltown community held no real enmity towards Watts School, but they were not heavily involved in the affairs of the school when Michael arrived. Michael insisted from the start that the oral history project had to reclaim the history of Walltown School, even though that history was potentially divisive. This decision, and his sponsoring of a Walltown resident for the PTA president, was a way of demonstrating that he was taking on the responsibility for taking care of Walltown as one of the communities of Watts School. Yet by taking care of Walltown, he was simultaneously indicating that there were limits on his taking care of the Trinity Park community.

This contradiction in caring was one of the most difficult to balance, involving a judgment by Michael that he must not just care for the politically powerful in the school. As Fisher and Tronto note, there is often a contradiction between the responsibility assumed in the judgment to take care of and the available power to accomplish caring. In Michael's case, assuming the responsibility for Walltown jeopardized his power to do so.

While a school principal's responsibilities in caring are rather diffuse, indirect, and at a distance from the children, this does not necessarily mean that the principal abdicates taking care of the children to the teachers. As indicated above, the teachers at Watts School viewed doing something good for the students as doing something good for themselves. The oral history project was one way Michael could show he was also taking care of the children. He was visible in classrooms and available to the children for conversations. He greeted them and bade them farewell each day. His indirect efforts, including his focus on improvement of teaching, meant that he took responsibility for helping develop new experiences for the students. The lesson, however, is that the contexts of caring for a principal are not as focused as that of a teacher or parent. The responsibility to take care of all the participants in the school means that, by design, the principal's role is always structured by trade-offs—trade-offs in how much effort can be given to any one constituency, in how much one's caring for some may enhance or diminish the power to care for others, and in how much the principal's caring burdens the teachers. In taking care of, aesthetic caring takes on new meaning. Rather than abstract, it may be better understood as diffuse and indirect.

CAREGIVING

Fisher and Tronto (1990, p. 43) write: "*Caregiving* is the concrete (sometimes called hands-on) work of maintaining and repairing our world." Clearly, here we see Noddings's distinction between aesthetic and authentic caring most dramatically. As above, the diffuse and indirect nature of the principal's responsibility to take care of gives way to even more indirect acts of caregiving. In traditional administrative logic, it is the principal's job to see that the teachers care for the students. Fisher and Tronto give a more substantive argument. They see caregiving as requiring extensive knowledge, experience, skill, and judgement, "a more detailed, everyday understanding" (p. 43), and "more continuous and dense time commitments" (p. 43) than those invested primarily with the responsibility to take care of. They also argue that caregivers typically suffer from limited resources of time, skill, knowledge, and funds, suggesting that a key role for those whose job tends to limit them more to aesthetic caring is to try to provide the resources caregivers need. However, in public schools, resources are relatively scarce and fixed. The principal's job then is to garner new resources and to develop flexibility with existing ones.

Developing new resources is always problematic for a school principal. In Michael's case, it was an ongoing struggle. Funds were not generally available, and time was largely fixed in that he could not reasonably ask the caregivers, the teachers, to give more of themselves than they already were—one does not do this to people about whom one cares. It seemed that the only way to help develop more time and funding was to try to develop cooperative projects with other local agencies. The university's involvement in the history project was the first step in creating a partnership with a host of projects that enabled others to devote time to school affairs. With the help of the university, numerous small grant proposals were written to try to generate funds, but to little avail. In the end, the only new funds developed were funding by the university's dean of education to help underwrite the oral history project, the funding of a playwright by the local arts council to turn the history into a school play, and a grant for the caring study. Clearly, grant funds were not available to help the primary caregivers. The PTA, with Michael's encouragement, held a number of fund raising events for monies that would be used to provide inservice training, books, supplies, and celebrations.

The resource of time was bolstered by similar arrangements. The university people donated their time to the various projects, trying to minimize the time commitments required of teachers. The PTA provided volunteers for numerous school activities, thus making movement beyond the classroom for educational experiences possible. Even with these efforts, though, it is clear that significant influxes of money and time to the caregiving by teachers was difficult to arrange.

Developing skills and knowledge to assist in caregiving was somewhat easier to arrange. With the PTA funds, the numerous staff development activities noted earlier helped teachers develop new skills and knowledge related to their teaching. The caring grant from the Lilly Endowment enabled a series of discussions of the concept of caring with the staff. As Michael observed, doing the classroom ethnographies for this study meant that teachers discussed and experimented with caring in ways they never had before. In three years, Michael was able to provide new skills and knowledge in the major content areas, in instructional delivery through cooperative learning, and in caregiving itself.

Even though resources were limited, Michael was able to provide considerable flexibility in their use. All of the above projects meant that the many everyday routines of school and classrooms were at issue. Instead of subjects being distinct, there was more cross-subject integration. The whole language training gave teachers more flexibility about how to structure reading and writing and its relationship to the other content areas. The oral history project led to an integrated social studies, music and drama experience for the children, crossing both content area boundaries and even the more sacred boundaries of individual classrooms. Teachers were also encouraged to experiment with new instructional ideas and to request ways the school could be more responsive to their needs in caregiving to the children.

However, it should be clear that the teachers were primarily giving care to the students; Michael was primarily giving care to the teachers. Even so, the separation of teaching from administrative roles in schools meant that he actually had limited time in interaction with the teachers. The diffuse and indirect responsibility of taking care of translated into diffuse and indirect caregiving.

CARE-RECEIVING

As we noted earlier, one of Michael's most difficult undertakings was to find out what the teachers would value as caring; the same was true of community members. Caring is reciprocal in that the definition is jointly constructed by the caregiver and care-receiver. As Fisher and Tronto discuss, this joint construction is often problematic. A shared understanding of the meaning of any event is difficult to develop, typically taking considerable time and interaction. Indeed, the shared understanding we think of as culture involves long processes of socialization and then offers no guarantee of harmony. Fisher and Tronto see developing a shared understanding being affected by power relationships that tend to shift the definition of what the care-receiver needs to what the powerful wish to provide.

Michael, of course, was in a position of power and did wish the school to improve. The key issue was whether the teachers and community would see his wishes as caring or as exercises of his authority. In retrospect, it is clear that they were perceived as both. There was no way to overcome the fact that Michael was the principal and an agent for state and local educational requirements. However, the teachers at Watts School were well accustomed to this role—for all principals have it as part of their job. What they were looking for was someone who would protect them from unnecessary demands for information, compliance, and increased work-loads. They understood that the principal had the power to mediate these demands.

Michael attempted to serve as a buffer. He tried to respond to information requests himself, rather than pass them on to the teachers. He took a stance on some initiatives, telling the teachers that they would not have to comply. He stalemated district requests for curriculum alignment initiatives, for example, when they came at a bad time for the teachers. His interest in improvement did require more teacher time—internal advisory council meetings, regular faculty meetings, inservice workshops, meetings related to the various projects, and so on. Yet he confined these meetings to the immediate after-school hours that teachers were required by regulations to stay in the building, and built other meetings into the day. He did ask teachers to try new curricula and implement cooperative learning, which added preparation time to their workload. Yet all in all, the teachers reported in interviews that they felt these were appropriate and demonstrated his commitment to the school. They were indications he cared about, and was taking the responsibility to take care of, that symbolic entity *the school.*

The teachers also were looking for someone who would listen to them about priorities. They wanted a principal who had the strength to be able to negotiate with them. Michael's initiation of the oral history project taught them that he wanted to learn before he acted, and that he wished to learn from them and the communities. The internal advisory council became the arena for the teachers to express their preferences and to negotiate what the priorities were. Power was shared here. Faculty meetings had some of this character, but as time went on they became more arenas for sharing ideas, distributing information, and bringing the internal advisory council's recommendations for review and action. The teachers communicated early on who their "lead" teacher was, recommending Michael check with her on less important issues. She became his sounding board for ideas, and Michael ended up designating her the "teacher-in-charge" of the school in his absence.

Finally, as we indicated above, the teachers defined themselves as being cared for when the principal was "doing something good for the children." In their minds, their own welfare was intimately linked to the welfare of the children. This, of course, is an indication of the altruism of the teachers. They were less concerned about their own needs—indeed they may have largely given up on the notion that the school and/or the principal could serve them or could fully care for them. They sacrificed a centering on themselves for a centering on the community.

The communities as care-receivers is a much more complex issue. First, the communities were not accustomed to the school doing anything directly for them other than fulfilling the institutional mission of educating their children. Trinity Park was clear that the school was central to the neighborhood's identity, but took the relationship no further than that. Walltown believed their school had died, and that they were now sending their children to Trinity Park's school. Second, since the school was becoming increasingly African-American, there was some tension between the communities about Trinity Park's domination of the PTA and the school in general. Third, communities themselves are even more diffuse than is even a principal's responsibility. The relationship between a school and its communities is best understood not as a primary connection between specific people, but as a plethora of weak ties that are nonetheless binding (Granovetter, 1973).

Michael had to make a choice in his *taking care of* phase. He decided Walltown was being denied a relationship with the school that it deserved. He made repeated efforts to connect Walltown more closely to the school. He went to Walltown church services. He required the school history to include the history of Walltown School and neighborhood. He supported Walltown parents for officers in the PTA, ending up with a Walltown parent as president for the last two years. A play was written and performed by students, teachers, and parents that highlighted the relationship of the two communities and the school over time and focused on the issues of segregation, desegregation, and race relations. This was a major community celebration for Walltown, widely attended and talked about. Walltown came to view Michael as caring for them, but this is still in process.

Trinity Park, of course, was not ignored in all this. Yet it was clear that Michael was trying to change the image of the school to one that served both communities well. Trinity Park was losing its power over the school. Michael has supported their neighborhood, has given it new voice in both the oral history and the play, and maintained close connections with members of the neighborhood. Such tight connections with the Trinity Park community enabled an impressive community mobilization that was instrumental in thwarting a state recommendation that the school be closed. Under Michael's leadership, the majority African-American Watts School has become tied with another elementary school, a majority white school, as highest on test scores in this urban district. The school had improved as power was being shifted to Walltown. In all, the Trinity Park neighborhood is less sure that their interests will automatically dominate in school affairs, but still consider the school as an icon of Trinity Park. They see Michael as caring about the school and their neighborhood, but not necessarily in a way they would have preferred him to care. The relationship here has become more political.

The students see much less of Michael than they do of their teacher. Depending on their age, they have different experiences and understandings of him. The children happily identify him as their school principal, hug him, and so on. But here we can also see how much the teachers are giving care to him. They have constructed a shared belief among the children that he is a principal who cares about all of them. As Fisher and Tronto would say, the care-receivers, the teachers in this case, have decided they are in a caring relationship with their principal. This phase, of course, is the last phase in Fisher and Tronto's theory, but, as they argue, it is actually better understood as intertwining with the other phases. This in turn sets off issues for all other phases, "caring about, taking care of, caregiving" (p. 40). Michael now finds himself trying to deal with the interplay of phases and changing sets of actors as students graduate to the middle school and their parents with them. Teacher turnover also brings in new actors. Caring for him has a new meaning. In his role, he cares aesthetically. When caring about symbols, images, ideas and abstractions, the principal is negotiating the meaning of caring in the school. Clearly, he has authentic caring relationships with some of his teachers, and some of the children and families, but his role limits the extent of this. His role is to set the context for caring, to pay attention to the more abstract issues that surround developing caring relationships. This level of aesthetic caring is a necessity if teachers are to find authentic caring a significant part of their role.

CONCLUSIONS

Fisher and Tronto have a powerful critique of bureaucratic caring, arguing that bureaucracies tend to define *caring* in ways that help the organization perpetuate itself, and tend to separate *caregiving* from *taking care of*. Clearly, this is true in education and at Watts School. In the larger school district, caring counted for little—the focus was on higher test scores, to the virtual exclusion of teacher–student relationships. Caring was also traditionally not one of the things that teachers discussed at the school. Michael was able to use his power and authority to initiate a dialogue about caring at the school. Similarly, care-giving at Watts School and most schools is the responsibility of the teachers who are mostly women and at the lowest rung of the organization. Their role circumscribes their participation in caring, just as Michael's role did his. Michael found that he had little choice but to attend to aesthetic caring, even as he found that he could also be a caregiver to the teachers, at least in some ways. The bureaucracy of schooling does distort caring to meet its needs and structure. This critique needs to be elaborated and be used as a way to reconsider how schools should be organized if caring is to be the central logic.

In the meantime, we must help give the people who work in such bureaucracies a place to start. To do this, we need to explore the mixes of aesthetic and authentic caring that existing bureaucratic roles may allow. Michael found that he could have some authentic caring relationships, and that thinking about aesthetic caring did help him discern how he could help the teachers with their more authentic caring. Moreover, it may be that aesthetic caring can be important for symbolic legitimation of authentic caring. When the school principal expresses caring in the abstract *and* promotes a dialogue about authentic caring among the teachers, the context of caring is dramatically altered. "Do something good for the children" becomes the logic for the school's activities, letting the bureaucratic logic recede to some degree. Michael could not stop fulfilling the responsibilities the school district had assigned him with his appointment to the principalship. He could, however, use his power to articulate caring as the purpose of the school and protect and support the teachers as they embodied authentic caring. The lesson is that, even in bureaucratic contexts, people can expand their caring beyond what is officially required. A principal can become a caregiver too. This is an important step in the consideration of bureaucratic limits on caring. It is through such acts that critique becomes embodied as change.

REFERENCES

Canter, L., & Canter, M. (1976). *Assertive discipline*. Seal Beach, CA: Canter and Associates.

Fisher, B., & Tronto, J. (1990). Toward a feminist theory of caring. In E. Abel
    & M. Nelson (Eds.), *Circles of care*. Albany, NY: SUNY Press.
Gilligan, C. (1982). *In a different voice*. Cambridge, MA: Harvard University
    Press.
Gilligan, C., Ward, J., & Taylor, J. (Eds.) (1988). *Mapping the moral domain*.
    Cambridge, MA: Harvard University Press.
Granovetter, M. (1973). The strength of weak ties. *American Journal of
    Sociology*, 78, 1360–1380.
Noddings, N. (1984). *Caring*. Berkeley, CA: University of California Press.
Noddings, N. (1992). *The challenge to care in schools*. New York: Teachers
    College Press.
Shulman, L. (1983). Autonomy and obligation: The remote control of teaching.
    In L. Shulman & G. Sykes (Eds.), *Handbook of teaching and policy*. New
    York: Longman.

Part III

Teachers And Student Teachers: Views Of Caregivers

Chapter 5

Context, Relationships, and Shared Experiences: The Construction of Teachers' Knowledge

Van Dempsey

Given the long history of romanticism surrounding our ideals of good teaching, it sounds almost trite to suggest that good teachers are the ones "who care," or have "good relationships" with their students. Yet in research and reform efforts of the past decade aimed at both informing and improving the ranks of teaching, little attention has been paid to the role of *human-ness* in teaching—to the context of connection and relationships between children and teachers in classrooms. As Eaker and Prillaman point out in the introduction to this book, recent efforts to portray the good teacher have focused almost solely upon issues of effectiveness such as teacher "competencies" and technical skills.

These directives in teacher effectiveness stand in stark contrast to the essentially intersubjective nature of teaching, and it is to this nature I wish to turn. Based upon conversations with 10 elementary school teachers, I suggest that good teaching is defined, to a great degree, by the context, relationships, and shared experiences that students and teachers construct in their classrooms. Much of the knowledge on which teachers rely in their work is constructed in those contexts, relationships, and shared experiences.

THE STUDY AND THE SETTING

Over the course of the academic year 1989–1990, I worked with a research team conducting an ethnographic study of the role of caring in an elementary school. Each of the six researchers on the study team spent one day per week observing classrooms in the school. These observations were conducted for the entire school year. I originally participated in the study by observing a fifth-grade classroom from September through December, and conducted interviews with the faculty in the spring. I participated in the "caring" study to facilitate my own study of teacher professionalism, and this was understood by the rest of the research team. Our trade was an extra series of classroom observations for them in exchange for access and technical support for me. I went into the study with caring as a clearly secondary concern, if indeed a concern at all. What I was genuinely interested in doing was a critique of recent reform efforts in the professionalization of teaching. My plan was to interview the faculty of the school and, along with the observations being done by the research team, come up with some ideas on how professionalization efforts might be bettered by grounding them in the everyday lives of teachers.

The setting of this study is Cedar Grove Elementary School, located near the central business district of Treyburn, a southern city of approximately 130, 000 people. The school is located in College Park, a middle-to upper-middle-class white neighborhood. The school also serves the children of Rougemont, a lower-class black community immediately adjacent to College Park. At the time of the study the school served 300 children (65% African-American and 35% white) from kindergarten through fifth grade. The faculty included 30 people—teachers, teacher assistants, and various specialists. Faculty tenure ranged from one year to 30-plus years. The school principal was in his third year. I conducted individual interviews with 10 teachers at the school. The process involved teachers representing kindergarten (Bess and Roberta), second grade (Pam), third grade (Serita), fourth grade (Martha), fifth grade (Amy and Sally), BEH (Becky), LD/EMH (Micki), and the media coordinator (Ann).

On the most recently reported CAT scores at the time of data collection in spring 1990, the school scored in the following percentiles on total test batteries: third grade, 55; fourth grade, 60; fifth grade, 58. These scores were at the top of the Treyburn City School District and in close competition with a neighboring school whose makeup was the opposite of Cedar Grove's. Cedar Grove has managed to achieve this level of educational success (by at least one criterion) in a system that—judged by many educational standards—does not do very well at all. The Treyburn City Schools, according to most recent reports, operate below state accreditation standards on the California Achievement Tests, post one of the lowest average SAT scores of any district in the state, and one of the highest dropout rates. In a recently released "Report Card" (January 1991, by the State Board of Education and the State Department of Public Instruction) of the 134 school districts in the state, Treyburn City Schools were rated "well below" standard when compared to other systems in the state with similar socioeconomic and demographic patterns. Cedar Grove's teachers, by this comparison, are "good" in a not so good district.

CONVERSATIONS WITH TEACHERS

In the interviews at Cedar Grove, I asked the teachers to discuss what they considered to be good teaching and good lessons, what they respect about teaching, and what they consider to be the most important elements and values of teaching. Each interview concluded with questions about what these teachers both give and get in their work and what keeps them in the classroom. Our discussions of these subjects centered upon their relationships with children and the contexts in which they teach. Again and again teachers described those who are "good" among their peers according to the nature of their *relationships* with children. The faculty at Cedar Grove discussed these relationships in terms of *caring, loving* children, *respecting* children, *being sympathetic, knowing* the children, and *understanding* the children.

Good Teachers: Relationships with Students

A Good Teacher Cares

All of the teachers with whom I talked believe that caring is an important element of good teaching. Ann feels that a good teacher cares, and that caring can be seen in the way teachers deal with students. Ann feels that caring is difficult to define. How would she know a caring teacher?

> If you asked me to name some I could. . . . But I think it's a—sometimes it's just a feeling. I think it's a way that you watch how a teacher interacts with her students. How the students seemingly relate to that teacher.

> I think it's just a kind of an intangible feeling that you get when you just watch a teacher with a class. And how they interact with the students (1/8)[1].

Martha also feels that good teachers "care about kids" (1/5). She feels that part of caring for students is valuing each person, and treating each one as someone important. In the process of caring, teachers have to create a caring environment.

> I think it's also a time when [students] need to be able to express feeling about things, but it's a real risky thing to do. So you have to care enough to create an environment where that's OK. Where it's safe to do that kind of thing in front of the other kids or in a small group or just, you know, one to one (1/7).

Martha does several things in her class to establish a caring environment. One of those things is spending a lot of time preparing to teach.

> I put a lot of time into finding what I hope are interesting, challenging, exciting ways to do things. So that even if you're planting seeds for the tenth time in your life, it's still new and different in some way (1/7).

Martha also shows her caring through physical contact—rubbing, tickling, hugging. Caring can mean, "just listening to each

---

[1]Code shows the interview/page number for each subject's quote.

other. You know, listening to what they have to say. And taking it seriously" (1/7). Caring teachers listen to things kids want to talk about, not necessarily things related to school. Caring teachers, to Martha, let students redo their work, so that students can do the best work they're capable of doing.

Martha also said that part of being a caring teacher is helping students learn to care for each other: "You have to, you have to care that other kids are accepting of each others' differences. And so you have to help kids care. You have to help kids take care of each other" (1/6). Children confirm their caring attitudes in the way they talk to Martha and interact with her: "The kids come up and hug me or walk around, holding, grab hold of your hand as you're walking by. You know, there's a lot of physical contact initiated on their part as well" (1/7–8).

Like Martha, Amy believes that a good teacher cares, and a caring teacher is one who listens. Amy said that communication is one way to show a child that, "Look, I do care."

> You know your time is limited. [There's] so much to be done. But there's, there's always a minute there that you can talk to a child and give him or her that attention that they need. It's a minute available, and it may be all they need is just that one minute to know that, well, she does care. She's not ignoring me (1/4).

Part of listening, according to Amy, is doing so even when you don't want to. "There are times when I really don't want to be bothered, but I know, well, you know, I have to. I have to" (1/5). That includes, as with Martha, listening to whatever they want to talk about: family problems, peer pressure, homework problems, best friend problems, personal problems. "Whatever they are talking about you need to listen to it" (1/5).

Becky feels that caring teaching means unselfish teaching. Caring also means being optimistic. As the Behaviorally and Emotionally Handicapped teacher, Becky believes that she has a unique perspective on caring as hope:

> [Teachers] care about a lot of things. They care about the future of our nation. They care about the individual kids. I mean, teachers have to be hopeful too. And see hope. I mean, I've also got a

different perspective from a lot of mainstream teachers, because I
look at the kids that are the throw-away kids (1/9).

As evidence to the caring in her classroom, Becky thinks that
people would see excited children and an excited teacher.

Getting excited with the kids when they are excited. I guess I'm a
pretty touchy kind of person. And I go up to a kid and help them
and you put your arm around them and you bend down to their
level. I keep up with what's going on in their lives (1/10).

Becky feels that teachers must deal with problems directly, but
with care. Children do have to know what is tolerable behavior.
Becky credits much of her students' positive response to discipline to their desire to move out of the BEH classroom; the
children understand that in order to do that, they have to exhibit
good behavior. As an example of a student understanding that
Becky's decisions are made out of a sense of care, Becky offered
me this story:

Well, one time one of the kids had just flown off up in the library.
And he was hitting other people and throwing shelves over and
stuff. And I had to put him into—do you know what a therapeutic
hold is? It's like the straight jacket. You have the hands down by
the hips and, I mean not up here [at the shoulders] because then
you could dislocate a shoulder. But down here and you're behind
them.

Anyway, so I've got this kid and I'm braced against a bookshelf.
And one of the kids said, "Oh gosh, look! Ms. [Becky] Kirby's got
Lamont!" I don't remember what the other kid said, but Lamont
said, "No, she's not trying to do anything. She just wants me to
calm down." Which was the exact truth, but I couldn't believe he
was that perceptive. And I think that that probably indicated that
he knew that I wasn't trying to hurt him, and that I wasn't trying
to be punitive. That I was just trying to help him to get control of
his own behavior (1/10–11).

Becky feels that sometimes, in the process of disciplining a
child, she might make a mistake or treat a child unfairly. In any
disciplining situation, particularly one where blame is difficult

to apportion, Becky said, "You have to explain why you did it. You've done it incorrectly in their eyes and perhaps in your own eyes. You say, 'You're right, it was a mistake'" (1/11). Part of this fairness is to not lie to the children, and when mistakes are made by the teacher, "to try to make amends for it" (1/11).

Good Teachers are Empathetic and Trusting

Serita describes a good teacher as one who empathizes with her students. She feels that when students realize the empathy of teachers, they gain more confidence in teachers. Students then know that teachers "feel their pain and their sorrow, or when they're hurt, or when they're happy" (1/5). Such empathy on the part of the teacher helps the teacher to understand the students better and understand why students do the things they do. "It helps bring about a better relationship, I think, between teacher and pupil" (1/5).

Being empathetic, as Serita said, helps teachers build understanding for students. Being understanding helps teachers cope with the variety of children that come into classrooms, whether that variety is due to cultural differences, differences in home situations, or simply to students just having a bad day.

> Well, [a good teacher] just understands that people get angry, or unhappy, and that the way you feel about things can affect the kind of work you do and the things that you do at times. But it's OK to be a real person. It's OK for a teacher to be a real person. It's OK for a teacher to be a real person. It's OK for kids to be, it's OK for the child to be angry. And learn ways to express that anger that aren't harmful to others (Martha 1/7).

Good teachers know children and know the circumstances from which those children come to school. Roberta feels that to know the children means that you know the parents: "A good teacher has to know her children's parents. You have to get parents in as soon as you can. If there are problems in the home I want to pick up on that" (1/3–4). Roberta gets to know her children by spending the first few weeks of school giving them activities to do that allow her to walk around the room talking to the children while they work. "I have lots of materials and what they use tells you a lot about them" (1/4).

Micki referred to knowing the children as being "connected" with them (1/9). She knows she connects by what she feels with the students.

> Well, after you know a kid, there's lots of things you can sort of, you feel it. You can tell by the look on their face, by what they say to you. A lot with younger children and older children, in older young people, by their body language. Body language I think, is one of the most under used things in the classroom, in classrooms. You can see people tense, you look at the eyes to see if they truly are figuring out a problem or not. You can watch (1/8).

Micki, in agreement with Roberta's comments on knowing the students, feels that it is important to know the students' home contexts. She feels that, after knowing the neighborhoods from which students came to school, she better knows her students. "And that helps me then to understand each individual" (1/8). Micki summed up her relationships with children this way:

> I have a certain ethic I think when I look at students and that is that my relationship with that student is a moral one and the moral responsibility is to make sure that they learn what they're supposed to learn.

> And you just, it's sort of embedded in that, and also in the context of it all. And it's so many factors that it's, it's something that's almost spiritual or metaphysical. It's really being in the flow, and being connected (1/9).

A Good Teacher Communicates

Good teaching requires the ability to communicate. Sally described that ability as:

> Well, I think one thing important is to be able to communicate with an age group you work [with]without talking down to them. I think, you know, they can kinda tell when you do talk to them as children. I really kinda think of 'em as just smaller people, and you know, try not to ever talk down to them. Because they're

really aware of a lot of things that you might not realize could be wrong. Children are pretty worldly. Probably more than you think they know about some things (2/1).

Sally continued that good teachers communicate in this "special way" (1/2), being able to get points across to students that other people couldn't get across, even using the same words.

Like Sally, Amy feels it important to communicate with children on their level, understanding that those things that children hold as important are part of their world as children. Amy feels that a good teacher communicates with the children and the parents as well, for it is crucial to constantly reassure parents that she is doing the best she possibly can for their children.

What I Give, What I Get, What Keeps Me Going

I concluded all my interviews by discussing with the teachers what they give and get out of teaching, and why they continue to do it. Some teachers feel they give students skills while they teach them. Ann feels that, in the media center, she gives students "skills" in finding information that they might not be taught after they leave elementary school. Micki feels she gives her students a love for the subject matter, and an interest in the world, and the motivation to understand it. Sally hopes that she gives her students "just basic good principles for living" (2/10).

Other teachers discussed what they give of themselves in purely emotional terms. For example, Pam gives, "Concern, love, patience, heart, soul, energy, empathy, sympathy, time, money" (3/2). Martha gives "Everything, there's nothing left" (2/1). Bess gives "enthusiasm to others" (2/12), and Ann gives "a little part of myself" (3/11).

What do teachers get back? Most of what teachers say they get comes directly from the students they are teaching. Many of the teachers referred to verbal and gestural responses from the students. Ann gets "Smiles and hugs and thank you's, and I really like that. And, gee, that was great—that was a great story" (3/11–12). Martha gets the same kind of satisfaction back from the students, with the accompanying hugs and kisses. She also learns from the students:

I get a lot of feedback. I get constant feedback about how I'm doing as a teacher and that helps me. Helps me grow and helps me change. So I sort of, I learn as much from them as I hope they learn from me (2/19).

Bess referred to this same interchange between teachers and students, but on the subject of having fun. "You know, if I'm having fun, I get into it in a much more fun kind of way. Which makes it much more enjoyable for them. So we're giving to each other, I hope" (1/9).

Becky, the BEH teacher, talked about what she gets back from her teaching in the context of the special students she works with:

From this group of kids, not much. You know, with some kids, a couple of kids, you see the little bits of progress here and there. I mean, you see them do something really appropriate with another kid. And you see them, you know, you see a kid smile for the first time in a week or something. And that's what I get back (2/7–8).

Finally, the teachers shared with me the things that keep them going. One motivation is the ability to create and to be creative. For Bess, this means the opportunity to try new things with new groups of kids. Similarly, Martha finds teaching to be stimulating and "an outlet for a lot of my creative energies" (2/19–20). For Martha, this is both a challenge and an opportunity for growth.

Ultimately, what keeps these teachers going are their experiences with "the kids." Bess sticks with it because "the kids are just super" (2/13). Pam and Sally keep going because of the sense of accomplishment in knowing they can help students learn. Amy said of her students, "I love every one of 'em. I really do" (2/13). Martha enjoys seeing the "little light in somebody's eyes start to shine because they've discovered something new or realized they could do something that they didn't think they could, or get excited about something. That gets me, too" (2/20). The children keep Martha going in another way:

When I see kids working together as a group. When they begin to care about each other as people and do spontaneous, kind, thoughtful things for each other, that always touches me (2/20).

"IN" THE CONTEXT

When first I conceived of the study of teacher professionalism I referred to above, I used the phrase *inside looking around* in its title as a play on how I, methodologically, would advance toward a theory of teacher professionalism. In moving toward a useful theory of teacher professionalism, I attempted to suggest how those who work in that aspect of educational reform would have to build, at least in part, on the everyday lives of teachers.

As the teachers and I progressed through discussions of good teachers, good lessons, teacher decision making, and other areas addressed by that study, the teachers consistently informed me throughout the interviews, that *people who don't teach, don't understand what it is to teach*. The teachers insisted that, to understand teaching, you have to teach. A conversation I had with Pam reflects this sentiment.

Van: Are there other things you respect about teaching?

Pam: The teacher-to-teacher relationships. We do a lot of *sharing* and *understanding* that other people don't understand.

Van: Who are those other people who don't understand?

Pam: People who are not teachers. If someone else could spend time in a classroom like Dr. Beard [study team member in her class] they could relate.

Van: What would you want a parent to see if they could observe your class?

Pam: One day won't do it. Even one week is not enough. You have to stay here to see the problems we deal with in the course of a year. But one day would show a lot. Parents stay thirty minutes and judge by that. It doesn't tell an awful lot. There are so many things to see.

Van: Do you have to teach to understand?

Pam: I think so. You don't necessarily have to teach but you have to be inside the classroom. The secretary is here but she doesn't know what's going on inside classrooms. You have to teach to know how to deal with it. Even assistants who stay in here all the time can't deal with the situation by themselves (1/3).

This desire to have parents and others see the work that teachers do consistently arose in the teachers' conversations with me. Teachers expressed not only an interest for the community to be "in" schools, but to participate in what goes on in classrooms. Some teachers, such as Ann, had seen in their own experiences the positive impact on the community's perception of teaching that bringing parents in created.

> Well, I think sometimes parents don't understand exactly the energy level at which you expend when you are with a group of kids from eight in the morning until 2:30 to 2:45 in the afternoon. One of the parents in, who has helped Martha and who frequently comes in here tells me that she just can't. The first couple of days that she was in there she was just exhausted (3/5).

Ann feels that the parents who spend at least some time in classrooms have a "feel" for what teaching is like (3/4–5). According to Bess, "I've always said the best way for the public, parents, anybody to learn about what a teacher goes through in a day is to come and spend time in schools" (2/11). Martha would like to see parents actually trying their hand at teaching, "And have them do all things I do" (2/19). But she also feels that simply getting parents into classrooms just to see what goes on everyday would be helpful.

Originally my study, entitled "Inside Looking Around: Toward a Grounded Theory of Teacher Professionalism," was an attempt to ground discussion of teacher professionalism in the everyday lives of teachers. My call for being "in" was to understand teaching as a profession from the context in which teachers work. But as I progressed through the study, "getting in" took on new significance for me. *Inside looking around* now was a *double entendre* for me: it included my being in as a researcher, but more importantly it raised to the surface the issue of what teachers "know"—and how they know it. What these ten teachers referred to in conversations with me, they referenced *contextually*. What they know about teaching, they know *contextually*. (And what ultimately makes teaching a profession can be found most directly in the context of their work.) What they want the public to know requires experiencing in some way what teachers experience. Teachers came back consistently to contexts and relationships and their under-

standing of and *knowledge from* the contexts and relationships in which they teach. Context and contextual knowledge arising from the relationships and shared experiences of their every-day lives drives their work. The fundamental aspects of what they know come from their experiences with children and other teachers.

As teachers defined *good teaching*, they focused first on the relational aspects of their experiences and then upon judge-ments of those relationships and experiences. For instance, good teachers care, love, respect, are empathetic, know children, and understand children. All of these attributes define the nature of experiences they have with children. Good teachers are also flexible, communicate, and establish fair and productive control with students (maintain effective discipline). Flexibility, com-munication, and control require judgements about their relation-ships and experiences with children.

In terms of what teachers give to teaching, what they get from teaching, and what keeps them in teaching, teachers almost unanimously refer to the experience of being a teacher and those relationships with children that are a part of that experience. Teachers cite their contribution to the relationships and experi-ences they share in teaching as what they "give." The rewards of those shared experiences and relationships—the hugs, kisses, and thank you's—are what teachers "get." That exchange is what keeps them going.

My conversations with teachers about public beliefs and misperceptions made the role of teaching's *context* vital to teachers' knowledge of their own work. The teachers credited the public's persistent misunderstandings of teachers and schools to that same public's pervasive ignorance of what goes on in schools on a day-to-day basis. The public's devaluing and misunderstanding is due to its lack of knowledge that teachers use every day. Teachers feel that the public doesn't understand teaching because they don't see teaching, literally or figura-tively. The only way the public can understand what teachers know is to *share* the experiences and relationships that teachers share and to be an ongoing part of the context of teaching. For the public to share in the knowledge of teaching, the public must come inside.

SHARED EXPERIENCES, CONSTRUCTED KNOWLEDGE

At the root of the teachers' discussion of their work is the idea of care—of connections and relationships between people. The issue of caring offers a fresh perspective on how we might look at the everyday lives of teachers. The caring literature's emphasis on context, connection, and relationships may provide us with new ground on which to examine just what the knowledge base of teaching is. The truly important knowledge that is produced in good teaching may be that knowledge that we *don't* know—and *can't* know—unless we are *in the context* in which it is created—the interaction between students and teachers.

My conversations with teachers have suggested to me two possible ways whereby consideration of caring offers opportunities for a better understanding of the everyday lives of teachers. First, an expanded discourse on caring may provide a deeper understanding of the relationships and interactions that occur in schools. Second, caring might help us to better understand the nature of teacher knowledge, and the importance of what we *don't* understand very well about what teachers do every day. A consideration of caring might also position discussions of teachers' work in terms of what teachers do, rather than in the currently rampant discussions of what teachers don't do. As McDonald states:

> I want to call special attention to two thematic threads. . . . One is that the experience of teaching involves a struggle for complex, and ultimately tenuous, control. A second is that as a result of this struggle there is an inevitable and morally legitimate tension between teachers and students. I believe that this struggle and its tensions are at the heart of . . . the uncertainty of teaching, its messy practicality, which theorists generally sidestep. (1986, p. 377)

We can take McDonald's comment as a subtle plea to stop sidestepping the messy practicality and focus attention on the intersubjective nature of teachers' work.

Teaching *requires* connection between students and teachers, an intimacy. Such connection cultivates an interdependency between student and teacher, or as Gilligan says, "a view of self and other as interdependent and of relationships as networks created and sustained by attention and response" (1988, p.8). Gilligan goes on to comment—in a way tellingly reflective of Cedar Grove's teachers' comments on the importance of relationships and context—that:

> Being dependent, then, no longer means being helpless, powerless, and without control; rather, it signifies a conviction that one is able to have an effect on others, as well as the recognition that the interdependence of attachment empowers both the self and the other, not one person at the other's expense. The activities of care—being there, listening, the willingness to help, and the ability to understand—take on a moral dimension, reflecting the injunction to pay attention and not turn away from need." (1988, p. 16)

The teachers at Cedar Grove Elementary School rely upon the constant generation of experiences for students that allow them to trust that teachers will be supportive. The ability of the teachers to involve themselves in the child's world—and in the child's success—measures to some degree the existence of caring in the experiences that students and teachers share. Noddings claims that "the test of caring" partly lies in "whether the free pursuit of his projects is partly a result of the completion of my caring in him" (1987, p. 337). This is a particularly strong point for teachers such as Martha, who wanted to make sure that her tenth lessons on seeds was as exciting as the children's first.

Attention, response, and communication—both physical and verbal—come together in the construction of an atmosphere of care for the teachers with whom I talked. For these teachers, this care is grounded in the experiences they share with their students, and they "know" it "through the experience of engagement with others" (Gilligan, 1988, p. 17). Knowledge constructed in these experiences by teachers (along with students) offers insight into a realm of teachers' knowledge that is rarely discussed. This tacit knowledge originates, develops, and emerges in the context of the experiences students and teachers share. And this knowledge can only be *fully* understand in the context of these experiences.

Belenky, Clinchy, Goldberger, and Tarule (1986), in a discussion of women's ways of knowing about their worlds and experiences, offer *constructed knowledge* as one perspective of women's knowing. These authors refer to constructed knowledge as "a position in which women view all knowledge as contextual, [and] experience themselves as creators of knowledge, and value both subjective and objective strategies for knowing" (p. 15).[2]Their work also draws a distinction between *separate knowing* and *connected knowing* (1986, p. 101). Separate knowing rests upon an "orientation toward impersonal rules," standards, and techniques of analysis, while connected knowing rests upon an orientation toward relationship, and conversation.

Belenky et al. expand their discussion of separate and connected knowing from work by Gilligan (1982) and Lyons (1983). Whereas Gilligan and Lyons speak of relationships between people, Belenky et al. include relationships between people and ideas, or between knowers and known (Belenky et al., 1986, p. 102). This expanded definition reflects the conversations about contexts and relationships as knowledge generated by the teachers and students at Cedar Grove School. Their contextual knowledge, based upon their experiences within the classroom, may be considered both constructed and connected—*cultivated in the shared experiences of students and teachers.* The extent of teachers' acceptance of the importance of this knowledge lies in the fact that all ten of the Cedar Grove teachers discussed both constructed and connected knowledge, with little or no attention to the "authority of experts," or externally produced knowledge (the *language of the technical* referred to in the introduction to this volume). "Connected knowing builds on the subjectivists' conviction that the most trustworthy knowledge comes from personal experience rather than the pronounce-

---

[2]This is contrasted with four other perspectives—*silence, received knowledge, subjective knowledge,* and *procedural knowledge.* These perspectives range from women seeing themselves as totally uninvolved in the production of knowledge (silence), through acceptance of externally produced knowledge (received), reliance only on subjective knowledge, and the application of objective procedures for learning and transmitting knowledge (procedural).

ments of authorities" (Belenky et al., 1986, pp. 112-113). For these teachers *truth* is that knowledge" that is personal, particular, and grounded in firsthand experiences" (p. 113).

In constructed knowledge and connected knowing, as presented by Belenky et al., Gilligan, Noddings, and the faculty of Cedar Grove School, empathy plays a vital role in establishing and maintaining relationships and enhancing shared experiences between students and teachers. For the teachers, coming to an understanding of the emotional, social, and psychological "location" of students enhances these shared experiences—in essence they are sharing the students' locations. Connected knowers "learn how to get out from behind their own eyes, and use . . . the lens of another person" (Belenky et al., 1986, p. 115).

In constructed knowledge and connected knowing, *"All knowledge is constructed, and the knower is an intimate part of the known"* (Belenky et al., 1986, p. 137). Conversely, and appropriately, the known is a part of the knowers and there resides. In the case of care for teachers, it resides as well with the students and in the experiences between teachers and students. And for teacher knowledge, it places what teachers construct as knowledge in a vital realm:

> To see that all knowledge is a construction and that truth is a matter of the context in which it is imbedded is to greatly expand the possibilities of how to think about anything, even those things we consider to be the most elementary and obvious. Theories become not truth but models for approximating experience. (p. 138)

Teachers' constructed and connected knowledge *lives* in their shared experience with students.

CONCLUSION

In one of my interviews with Micki, she talked about knowing when to push kids—to motivate them to work and succeed. I asked her, "You said that you have to know when to push, when to leave alone, when to hug. How do you know those things?" Micki responded:

Hunches. You just, you just do it. I mean, I don't know. I've tried to figure that out. But it's almost like you get a feeling, you try it, and if it doesn't work you back off. I don't know how to describe this (1/8–9).

Micki's response provides a good example of the seeming enigma of the knowledge on which the teachers at Cedar Grove based their work. The possibilities inherent to the mystery of her answer are powerful for enhancing our understanding of teaching, but we are required to turn our attention from the technical aspects of teaching to the intersubjective, at least for a while.

I have attempted, through the commentary provided by the teachers of Cedar Grove Elementary School, to take a glimpse at the intersubjective, and to provide an "alternative conversation" on the nature of good teachers and the knowledge with which they work. Connections, relationships, and caring are very much a part of the knowledge base of teaching, but it is a part that our reform efforts have thus far ignored. The teachers of Cedar Grove Elementary School define their work through their daily working lives, and they do so, at least in their conversations with me, at the exclusion of the "language of the technical." Such emphasis by these teachers invites us into a discourse such as that suggested by Belenky, Gilligan, and Noddings. Our opportunity is to examine teacher knowledge as constructed in context, relationships, and shared experiences.

REFERENCES

Belenky, M., Clinchy, B. M., Goldberger, N. R., & Tarule, J. M. (1986). *Women's ways of knowing: The development of self, voice, and mind*. New York: Basic Books.

Carnegie Forum on Education and the Economy. (1986). *A nation prepared: Teachers for the twenty-first century*.

Gilligan, C. (1982). *In a different voice: Psychological theory and women's development*. Cambridge, MA: Harvard University Press.

Gilligan, C. (1988). Remapping the moral domain: New images of self in relationships. In J. V. Ward, J. M. Taylor, & B. Bardige (Eds.), *Mapping the moral domain: A contribution of women's thinking to psychological theory and education* (pp. 3–20). Cambridge, MA: Harvard University Press.

Lyons, N. (1983). Two perspectives on self, relationships, and morality. *Harvard Educational Review, 53* 125–145.

McDonald, J. P. (1986). Raising the teacher's voice and the ironic role of theory. *Harvard Educational Review, 56* (4), 355–378.

Noddings, N. (1987). An ethic of caring. In J. L. DeVitis (Ed.), *Women, culture and morality* (pp. 333–372). New York: Peter Lang.

Chapter 6

Wanting to Care and Hoping to Control: An Exploration of Student Teachers' Relationships with Students

H. James McLaughlin

CONTINUING A CONVERSATION ABOUT CARING

One of the primary motivations for prospective teachers is their desire to care about students. Yet while educators have paid much attention to technical teaching skills or to enhancing cognitive strategies, little time has been spent exploring what it means to imagine and to enact caring. In both modern educational theory and university research agendas, there has been a predominant emphasis on the individual. The language of the self—self-efficacy, self-esteem, self-concept—fills journals of educational psychology as well as magazines for educational practitioners.

Partially in response to this overwhelming emphasis on self-fulfillment and individual achievement, Noddings (1984, 1986) has called for an "ethic of caring" in teaching. She has focused on the need for fidelity in teaching, which is predicated on being "reflectively faithful to someone or something" (1986, p. 496). Noddings defines fidelity as a way of being in relation to students "that supports affection and steadfastly promotes both the welfare of the other and that of the relation" (p. 497). Fidelity is not a duty bound to law or principle; it is a willingness to promote the growth of the other. For Noddings, "An ethic of caring guides us to ask, What effect will this have on the person I teach? What effect will it have on the caring community we are trying to build?'' (p. 499).

In considering how one's actions may affect others, Noddings opts for confirmation, rather than mere acceptance or criticism of the other. Teachers confirm students by acknowledging growth, even as they insist that students strive to do their best. Doing one's best requires self-examination: teachers should enable students to examine their own ways of acting and thinking. And doing one's best is not only an individual enterprise. Confirmation of students encompasses the social goal of teaching students how to care for others as part of building a caring community.

Alan Tom (1985) argued that teaching is a "moral craft," and not merely a technical concern. Liston and Zeichner (1987) tried to further explain the nature of moral deliberation in teaching. They used Noddings's distinction between an *ethic of duty*, which "utilizes abstract principles to assess day-to-day situations," and an ethic of care which "gives less emphasis to the type of principled reasoning entailed in an ethic of duty and more emphasis on ruminating over how one should be with students" (Liston & Zeichner, 1987, p. 4). "The focus is not so much upon the act of thinking as upon the actuality of being, on engendering particular dispositions or ways of being. Teachers can be honest, caring, and fair in their relationships with students, and they can encourage their students to act likewise" (p. 6). For Liston and Zeichner an ethic of care is a subset of an ethic of virtue. They stress the "elemental importance of commitment to a central core of moral virtues" (p. 7). There is no denial of duty or virtue: "Both an ethic of duty and an ethic of virtue are important for the moral education of teachers" (p. 4).

In several recent studies, teachers with varying levels of experience placed caring for others at the center of teaching (Kleinsasser, 1989; Linkous, 1989; Prillaman, 1988). Educators exploring the nature and the implications of caring share the belief that teaching embodies a personal caring relationship with learners. Such a relationship is problematic to novices, for they want to assume an authoritative professional role that may conflict with their ideal of being a caring person. Novice teachers, including student teachers, want to fulfill their "duty" *and* to care. In trying to enact caring they are forced to face questions of when and how to control classroom interactions. It is at the confluence of caring and controlling that some substantive problems of teaching well up.

EXERTING CONTROL

The purpose of this chapter is to continue a conversation about the nature of caring as it is enacted in classrooms, with a special focus on the tensions between caring and controlling. Controlling—often termed *discipline* or *classroom management*—is very important to student teachers and to many teacher educators. Student teachers are essentially visiting someone else's classroom; it is not surprising therefore that they worry about controlling an environment not of their own making. A number of studies have examined student teachers' efforts to exert control. Overwhelmingly, researchers have found a tendency for student teachers to become more "custodial" or controlling of students' behavior (Goodman, 1985; Hoy, 1969; Hoy & Rees, 1977). Beginning with Iannaccone's (1963) study, researchers have also indicated that student teaching contributes to an "instrumental perspective," a desire to simply make it through the experience by settling for "what works" in the short term (Gaskell, 1975; Gibson, 1976; Petty & Hogben, 1980; Popkewitz, Tabachnik & Zeichner, 1979). Sitter (1982) found in her study of elementary student teachers that they conceived of their role as a "junior partner" in the classroom. The student teachers tried to "prove themselves." They had four objectives—to develop teaching proficiencies, to attain leadership/control, to modify personal propensities, and to acquire a teacher identity. In another study, secondary language arts student teachers asserted that their primary aim as student teachers was "ownership" of the classroom (Kleinsasser, 1989). Being both student and teacher, they felt the need to establish themselves in a teacher role—to control the environment and their students' behavior— more than the need to learn about better ways to teach.

There seems to be an emphasis on controlling and a lack of focus on caring in the themes. In Tardif's study (1985), four secondary student teachers likewise expressed their need to "secure control" and were surprised at the difficulty of that task.

> Where previously the student teachers had felt that if they were well organized, respectful, just and courteous towards the students and knowledgeable in their subject field they would have few disciplinary problems, actual encounters with some classes of students left them feeling disappointed and at times disillusioned and deceived. (p. 145)

The student teachers in that study became more controlling as time went on, in line with the earlier cited studies. Tardif found that taking a role and securing control worked hand-in-glove. As student teachers tried to establish their authority and "teaching identity," they tried to create more "distance" from students and to adopt more stringent consequences for student misbehavior. Yet they wanted to be "firm but friendly." Their need to control conflicted with desires to care by "establishing a relationship" with students. Control won out: "The constraints of student teaching did not allow for the construction of a personal classroom reality by the participants" (p. 143).

Perceived Conflicts between Personal Relationships and Professional Roles

Some educators recognize the push-and-pull of personal relationships and professional roles. They assert that novice teachers enter their student teaching with an emphasis on concerns of the self, such as their personal connections with students. Then, as student teachers, the novices move through "stages" that lead to a greater concern with teaching tasks and eventually with student academic learning (Fuller, 1969). The suggestion is that a preoccupation with personal relationships conflicts with the need to accept a professional role (Buchmann, 1989; Moon, Niemeyer, & Karls, 1989).

Several researchers have found that controlling does not always take precedence over caring. Goodman (1988) examined 12 elementary student teachers' "professional perspectives." He determined that the students organized a practical philosophy of teaching around two perspectives: "Teaching as the Facilitation of Children's Growth" and "Teaching as a Problem of Control." These perspectives parallel the concerns with caring and controlling in my study.

Regarding the problem of control, most of the student teachers in Goodman's study strived for "institutional authority," the authority attached to one's role. To that end, they used the school's discipline system and tended to define particular children as the "problem." A small group of student teachers wanted to enact "personal authority," based on their personal relationships with the children. The student teachers in Goodman's study aimed to be both "friend" and "teacher," and found that quite difficult to do. Yet some of them held to that aim throughout student teaching.

Prillaman's (1988) study of 13 elementary student teachers and their cooperating teachers also examined the connections of caring and controlling. She found that student teachers held two negative stereotypes of teachers: the authoritarians and the incompetents. The former controlled classrooms too harshly; the latter were too lenient. None of the student teachers believed they were authoritarian or lenient. They equated being a "real teacher" with forming a relationship with students, which would of necessity include controlling in the classroom. As in Goodman's study, the student teachers also wanted to further their students' personal development. Those desires were supported by the cooperating teachers, who "consistently expressed that concern, commitment, and relating to the children were the hallmarks of being a teacher" (p. 96). As the term progressed, the student teachers in Prillaman's study devoted more time to talking or writing about discipline and control, a finding in line with previously cited studies. The student teachers moved from talking about the children to discussing their planned activities and the materials they would use (p. 113). But as Prillaman wisely pointed out: "This focus on activities and materials may not reflect a lack of concern for pupils. Instead, it may be a concern for pupils which motivates the emphasis on planning" (p. 114). Most student teachers seem to aim for "just surviving."

But student teachers in Goodman's and Prillaman's studies wanted to continue caring, even amid the travails of student teaching.

Part of the equation missing in prior studies of controlling is the complex factor of how student teachers attempt to care and to enact their ideals of being a person in the classroom, even as they try to control classroom events. Tabachnik and Zeichner (1984) acknowledged the studies showing a movement toward instrumentalism and controlling. But in their study of 13 elementary student teachers, "student teaching did not result in a homogenization of teacher perspectives" (p. 33). In fact, the student teachers' perspectives most often did not change from the time they began student teaching (see also Cole, 1985). One's long-held images of teaching as acts of caring do not simply dissolve in the course of trying to control in classrooms.

In this chapter I challenge the notion that developing personal relationships is somehow separate from one's professional role, and that one ought to move away from the personal and toward the professional if one is to be a good teacher. I first examine three student teachers' intentions to care and control prior to student teaching, and describe their ensuing actions in the classroom. A concluding discussion highlights the conflicts and the complementarity of caring and controlling.

METHODOLOGY

Data for the chapter were derived from an interpretive study of three middle-grades student teachers. The participants in the study were females ("Daria," "Jackie," and "Kerry" are their pseudonyms), 21–23 years of age, who were chosen because of their representative gender and age (young female undergraduates), their disparate backgrounds (varying socioeconomic status and parental occupations), and their expressed interest in the research project. My role in the study was that of a researcher; I had no connection with the participants' university coursework or their student teaching supervision. There were three data sources: observations, discourse, and documents.

Observations took place during student teaching in Spring

1989. There were six to seven observations of each participant in a teaching setting. Observational fieldnotes included descriptions of verbal interactions, behavior, and physical descriptions of the room. The fieldnotes were essential for subsequent conversations with the student teachers, in which they freely discussed their uncertainties while teaching.

Discourse with the participants included group and individual interviews and informal conversation. During the fall of 1988 there was an introductory personal interview with each participant. The questions in this semistructured interview focused on the participants' biographical data, their reasons for becoming a teacher, and how they might respond to the possible problems they foresaw occurring in student teaching. In Spring 1989 I attended six sessions of a teaching methods course. Following the classes, we discussed what the participants were learning and their concerns about student teaching.

The Methods course took five weeks of the term; the remaining ten weeks were devoted to observations of student teaching. In postobservational interviews, student teachers recollected their actions by describing and interpreting classroom events. The interviews were openended, fueled by an initial set of questions: "What happened in the period? What were you thinking when. . . .? Why did you act in that way? What alternatives might you have had?" The student teachers also projected their future intentions to act: "What will you do? What might happen if. . . .?" The purpose of the interviews was not to ascertain whether the participants could accurately recall classroom events, nor were the interviews meant to compare my interpretations with theirs. There were two purposes: to enable the student teachers to think carefully about what had transpired, in order to improve their teaching; and to enable me to examine the students teachers' inquiries about classroom interactions. All interviews were audiotaped and then transcribed verbatim.

I held final personal interviews with the three participants, their university supervisors, and the three cooperating teachers. The participants recounted how they felt about the student-teaching experience and what they had learned from it. The supervisors looked back on experiences as novice teachers, and commented on the student teachers' actions in response to classroom problems that arose during the term.

Documents comprised participants' biographical data, their written goals for student teaching, a syllabus and other materials from the teaching methods course, and personal journals kept by the participants (a university requirement). Participants made at least two entries each week, in which they described and analyzed classroom events. All three participants permitted me to read their unedited journals.

Several coding systems were used to make analytical passes through the data. After the final recoding, I wrote profiles of each participant that summarized accounts that best represented the participants' intentions and actions of caring and controlling. The accounts chosen involved incidents or issues addressed by the participant in multiple data sources. The profiles were then compared. Frequent phrases, strongly worded imagery, and responses that seemed to contradict or challenge prior statements were noted. Recurrent themes within and across profiles, phrased as much as possible in the participants' language, formed the foundation for inferential interpretations of data.

INTENTION AND ACTION

After analyzing data from my study, I believe caring was enacted in four ways: by modeling caring actions for students (*caring as self-portrayal*), by establishing personal relationships outside of class (*extracurricular caring*), by engaging in a curricular dialogue with students (*curricular caring*), and by creating a classroom community (*communal caring*). These categories were not developed a priori; they emerged from my interpretations of data as I searched for the substance of the participants' responses to classroom uncertainties. The categories represent a schema for thinking about the intentions and actions of caring, not the facade of a reified structure.

I will now introduce each participant through a brief biography and a description of her intentions—before student teaching—to care and to control. After discussing their intentions, I will explore the conflicts which the participants experienced as they attempted to teach. The summaries attempt to represent how the *participants* defined caring and controlling, whether or not their understandings reflected each category or accorded with theoretical notions.

Kerry

Kerry was 21 when I met her. She had spent her precollege years in a large city and had attended schools in an affluent area of town. Kerry was European-American. Her high school was large (a graduating class of 480).

Kerry was not particularly studious or academically motivated in the early years of college. She had done moderately well on her SATs coming out of high school, but her college GPA was just above average. Kerry attributed her mediocre grades to too much socializing.

Her mother was a long-time kindergarten teacher, and her father edited an educational publication, so she had grown up hearing about educational issues. She was quite aware of the influences on her decision to teach: "My whole family knew that's where I should go [into teaching]. Subconsciously, I have thought about it for a long time. I love teaching" (10/11).[1]

Intending to Care

> Kerry: (Responding to a question about why she does the work in a certain college class): Because I admire her. . . . Because it's fun. . . . This is challenging, but it's not out of reach. I want to be a teacher like her. I want to be a person like her. I'm more motivated to do well with her.(10/13)

To Kerry, caring originally meant to be both a person and a teacher, because to her, teachers were persons who cared about students and who in turn were respected and cared about. Caring was manifested in several different ways.

---

[1]Code shows the month/day of each interview.

Kerry: She [an English professor] shows interest in students outside of class. She's just so human. It is easier for students to relate to teachers who don't put up fronts. . . . She's so fair; she hasn't picked out a favorite. Nobody's ever given a wrong answer in there. She's not intimidating, and she has a desire to learn from us.

Researcher: How would you act in the classroom, if you were teaching now?

Kerry: I care a lot. I wouldn't be intimidating, and I would learn from the kids. I could do these things in the classroom right now. With practice, and lots of planning (10/13).

A teacher who was a person came to know students outside of class time, which constitutes *extracurricular caring*. She acted "human" and did not "put up fronts," an example of *caring as self-portrayal*. To Kerry, portraying oneself was also reflected in a willingness to trust spontaneous actions. She felt a need to make well-reasoned decisions while teaching: "[One must be] able to know when that track, that outline, is not going the right way. Then you're able to think on your feet. And decide 'Hey, this isn't doing it; what can I do, right now?'" (11/28). This ability to break from routines, to get off the track and determine "what to do, right now," was crucial to her notion of good teaching.

Kerry also cared about student learning, a mark of *curricular caring*. A good teacher did not intimidate students and indeed learned from them in a reciprocal relationship. In order to learn, one had to be "totally open-minded, prepared to make mistakes" (10/27). Kerry expressed her curricular intentions through a juxtaposition relating curricular content and process.

Researcher: Why teach middle grades?

Kerry: Because I had two of the most wonderful teachers. They would fit in here [the university]. Really caring. It takes more to be real, not just intellectual. . . . To care more about kids than what they learn, sometimes. If they learn how to study, how to deal

> with things at home, then I'll feel really good about
> my job. And in the process, if I can teach them a lot,
> that'll be icing on the cake. It's not necessarily what
> you teach them, but how you teach them. You're a
> role model. (10/27)

By caring for kids, she meant being more concerned with process (the *how*) than with content (the *what*). A key aspect of caring about learning involved not just telling, but getting students to think:

Kerry: I think about what my mom does. The human side of it—maybe a frustrated side. I see teachers as a person who tells you things, even education professors, not as a person. They don't ask us to think; you aren't put in that position . . . [This professor] doesn't come in with prepared lectures. She is prepared, and can lead the lecture, but starts with "What do you think? . . ." She rephrases questions, and comes back to a previous line of thought. (10/13)

In these passages Kerry equated caring for students with being real. She construed the problem as one of choosing between caring and learning, if learning were limited to content. In looking back at college she believed she had opted for social life over intellectual or academic life. In thinking ahead to student teaching, she aimed for being real rather than being intellectual.

Possible Conflicts with Caring

Kerry: You've always heard that it's easier to, yeah, that you should start off being strict and then be able to slacken off. But I just want to run in and have them all love me the first day, and I know what's gonna happen. I'll say, "Well, you can talk, and jump around. Do you like me?" . . . Then halfway through the semester I'll be able to create no order. (11/28)

This passage illuminates basic problems of caring and controlling. Kerry wanted to love the students and to be loved in return.

She foresaw a possible conflict with two kinds of control—control over student behavior (maintaining "order"), and self-control. Maintaining order required that one be strong. "I'm gonna have to learn to be strong and not give in. . . . And not try to appeal to their feelings all the time" (11/28). And Kerry understood that there can be problems with spontaneity:

> Kerry: You have to think before you speak. Because the students are going to take every word you say as gold, as if that's the truth.
>
> Researcher: Do you think teachers can think too much? Are there times when it's not a good idea to think?
>
> Kerry: I don't think we should get so caught up in evaluating every decision we make, every instant or everything that comes up, because you can't be creative. You lose your continuity. But at the same time, I know for me it will be very valuable to think at all times. (*All laugh.*) If you try to teach a lesson in a way that offends a race, or if you sputter out something that might offend someone that doesn't have a lot of money, I mean, in that case I don't think you can think too little.(11/28)

Spontaneity was for Kerry a part of being real, a sign of caring about students. But at times spontaneous action might result in not controlling oneself enough. In this sense "thinking on your feet," a means of thoughtfully controlling one's actions, embodied caring for students.

Enacting Caring and Controlling

Kerry's proclivity to spontaneity sometimes did not jibe with the demands of responding to 20-some students. Initially, Kerry used the phrase *losing it* as a positive description of *self-portrayal* that did not involve controlling. She offered the following account of an early class session where she lost it.

> Kerry: Today I lost it. I mean, it was Friday, I was silly, they were silly, we had a blast. They probably didn't have enough time-on-task, but Ms. _____ [the cooperating

> teacher] wasn't in the room, and we had a good time, and they did do stuff.
>
> Researcher: When you say you "lost it," what do you mean?
>
> Kerry: Well, I was giggling and they were giggling and we were having fun. When I told them they needed to— I said, "Okay, we've all got to calm down now." I said, "we're all getting out of hand; I know it's Friday but we need to get some stuff done." We played "boo-hiss"—and this was bad—I know we shouldn't have done it.

It was as if Kerry were playing at being a teacher, the sort of teacher she would want to be, while the cooperating teacher was away. We continued:

> Researcher: What's "boo-hiss"?
>
> Kerry: I would ask who had done their work. I would go (*affecting an announcer's deep voice*) "and the big survey says," and those people would clap and the ones who hadn't done their work would get it [booed]. . . . We were just all being silly and I'm glad Ms. _____ wasn't there. . . . To me, sixth graders that can work independently for an entire week and not blow it, that's good. They deserve to be able to—I mean, we turned out the lights at the beginning and all took 10 seconds and a big breath, and they thought that was funny. We calmed down and I left the lights on dim so they could manage to stay a little bit under control, and we opened the doors. (3/17)

Kerry "lost it" and then tried to alter the environmental conditions in order to enhance the possibility of student self-control. She talked often about "noise," "commotion," and other aspects of student behavior that she felt compelled to control. Kerry acted to control by rearranging the room, by trying out a system of penalties that included detentions, by nonverbal signals such as flicking the lights to get attention, by attaching grades to group activities, and by keeping students engaged in class activities.

"Losing it" can also assume a more negative connotation, related to the loss of control over one's emotions. No matter how students might react, Kerry aimed for self-control, which she believed was related to control over students.

> Kerry: I don't want to yell, and I find myself raising my voice so I can hear. So I try—when I tried it second period it didn't work today; sometimes it does—just being quiet (*speaks quietly*). And sitting down, or— I sat down one time second period. . . .
>
> Researcher: Is that what you do with those kids, when you feel like you're getting annoyed? Do you try to stop yourself, or slow yourself down?
>
> Kerry: If they're really causing a problem, I try to be quiet. But it's for me, it calms me down, and some classes it calms them down, too. To just be quiet. But it's for me, it calms me down, and some classes it calms them down, too. To just be quiet. Because there's some kids in each class that'll get annoyed enough with the rest of the class, they'll say, "Shh-shh, be quiet, Ms. K's tuned" [upset]. (3/11)

Kerry's efforts to "chill out" were in effect a sort of meditation; the intention was to quiet herself down instead of responding out of anger. For Kerry, self-portrayal as an act of caring in classrooms required self-control.

With regard to dilemmas of *extracurricular caring*, early in her student teaching Kerry followed the path set in the fall. She focused on individual students, making personal reciprocal connections. Personal affection—"liking him"—initiated her interest in helping Kevin, a seemingly bewildered student.

> Kerry: [Kevin would] never turn in a homework assignment, he's failed everything. I told Ms. _____ [the Cooperating Teacher] the first day I was in there, I said, "What's it with Kevin?" I've just taken a liking to him. There's nothing to like about him, except that he looks like he's in second grade and he should be in sixth. And he's very *innocent*. I mean, he's kind of just dingy, he doesn't know. But I mean the

little kid is *dear* . . . Anyway, so I decided—self-consciously I didn't know this—that he was gonna be my . . .

Researcher: Project?

Kerry: My project. And for some reason he walked into class, I guess it was Monday, and said something about "got any homework, Ms. ____ ?" And I said, "Kevin, Kevin, are you gonna study for your test tonight?" Because they have a little grammar test. And he, "Ohh," he went running back to his locker, and he found his grammar book. I said, "Do you have your notes on the sentence patterns?" "Oh, I didn't take no notes on the sentence patterns." (*She imitates Kevin's voice.*) And I said, "Kevin, study the pages you did for homework." "I didn't do no homework." I said, "Kevin, just take your book home, at least you can study *it*." Well, I was going, "Right, Kevin." He made an 85. . . . He just sailed through everything. I have never been so excited. I ran and got him out of Science to tell him he made an 85.

Kerry had not made a reflective judgment or a plan that this was the best of several possible actions, but she decided to make Kevin feel good about himself. She wanted to confirm him. Kevin had become her "project" because he was "dear" and he so obviously needed help.

Kerry saw a conflict between her desire to know students personally and her efforts to control in the classroom. She worried about "being mean" and was unwilling to change her informal approach to classroom interactions with students. At the same time she experimented with ways to control the behavior of several students whom she perceived as disruptive. Kerry was at first pleased that she was acting "firm" and not "mean."

Kerry: [The university supervisor] made me feel really good yesterday. I felt like I was overdisciplining them when I finally had to say, "Chill, cut it out." And she was like, "Kerry, you were just firm, you weren't

mean, you weren't angry, you didn't look that way."
And I felt so good. The way I want to do is, I sit with
them at lunch. I can't stand sitting with the teachers.

But then in class I've been trying to joke around
and make it lighthearted. But if they can't deal with
it, if they get out of hand, I guess I'll try to be firm.
And if they don't get it I make an example of one of
them, and I haven't had a problem after that. I mean,
I keep hearing the little theory about you've gotta be
mean at the beginning, and you've gotta be terrible
and then lessen up, lighten up. And that's probably
true, and I'm probably gonna get slapped in my face
again. But I haven't lost them yet. (3/17)

She recognized that there were possible problems associated
with her approach—"trying to joke around and make it light-
hearted." Kerry depended on her personal relationships with
students to help in controlling, and she felt it was working. Later
in the term she did lose it; she got angry and acted mean,
according to her own standard. She defined the difficulty as
being "too nice" at first, and then having to get mean in order to
control some unruly students. She was troubled by her lack of
self-control, and by constant efforts to maintain calm.

Kerry: I guess that's why I'm so frustrated now: because I'm
              not acting the way I want to act in the classroom.
Researcher: Why is that? Why aren't you acting the way you
              want to act?
Kerry: I think I'm fed up partially. I'm tired of getting-
              the-noise-down thing. I'm tired of people coming up
              to me and pestering me about things they need to
              make up or work they need to do. I'm very, very
              tired of the way fifth period treats me as a person.
              Maybe that's my big theme. I want to treat them as
              people and I want them to treat me back with
              respect, and I haven't gotten it. Instead of taking an
              extra grip and maybe a new step, I've just gotten the
              "wash my hands of it" attitude. I've only got 4 more
              days left. (5/3)

Kerry wanted students to be able to control their own actions.
Teachers should challenge students to be responsible, and they

should not have to put up with students' irresponsibility. While earlier Kerry had tried not to be "mean," and had even expressed ambivalence about being "firm," she changed her tune with the fifth period class:

Kerry: Can you tell I'm getting more cynical? Meaner?

Researcher: Are you?

Kerry: Fifth period hates me. I love it. If they hate me, it means they're going to be good. You really need to come see me in another class. I'm not nearly the ogre that I am.

Researcher: The ogre, huh. Another word that you've used a lot—

Kerry: Is *bitch*.

Researcher: (Laughs) No, you haven't used that one too much and you always speak more quietly into the tape when you do it. One word that you used before that is a common word in my ears with student teachers, which is *mean*. There's this thing about *mean*.

Kerry: . . . I feel like I've been mean instead of firm. Maybe that's because I skipped *firm* at the beginning and skipped on over to *mean*. I should have been firm all along and I would never have had to have been mean.

Researcher: You skipped *firm* and went on to *mean*. I like that. What a great turn of phrase that is . . .

Kerry: "She Skipped *Firm* and Went to *Mean*."

The researcher and Kerry were playing with the idea of being mean and being firm. She wished she had been firm from the start, because she believed the consequence of being nice was to end up being mean. But even though she bawled out the students in fifth period, Kerry still held to her notions that it was imperative to be firm and not mean.

Kerry persistently tried to enact *curricular caring* about groups or classes by actively engaging students in discussions and by synchronizing the class with their interests. She tried group work on several occasions, held ongoing discussions about current events, and built many lessons around topics that she felt would interest young adolescent students. Regarding the purpose of the class, Kerry several times encouraged students to "make connections to your own life" (3/5), a theme carried over from preteaching statements.

Caring was newly reflected in Kerry's high expectations of students' behavior and academics. She had seen how the tracking system relegated certain students to a prescribed curriculum and lockstep teaching methods. Initially, Kerry had frequently parroted the comments of the cooperating teacher, both during the interviews and in her journal. But at the last of the term she was considering the complexities of the structured tracking. In the final group interview, the three participants discussed how they felt about the various tracked groups of students. Kerry had taught "average" and "gifted" classes— here was her account of dealing with average students' needs:

Kerry: See, first of all, you don't do like I feel the teachers at [this school] do, where you break them off as— you've got four-level classes in Language Arts, anyway. And you say, "The advanced and the AG kids will do this, and the basic and average kids will do this." The average kids don't need to be doing basic work. If anything they need to be doing what the advanced kids are doing and just altering the way you teach it.

Researcher: . . . So what do we do with these average kids?

Kerry: I don't know, because they're the ones I have the trouble with. Discipline-wise. Like in the beginning, no matter what kind of teacher you are, you have to teach them how to be a good student. Teach them study skills or be very, very structured with them. Don't give them a way that they can be screw-offs. And then hold to it. And then, when they've got that part down, they obviously now ought to be able to do the fun stuff that the advanced kids get to do.(5/3)

Kerry discussed starting out with control and working into curricular caring, at least caring in terms of *having fun*. Notice how this mimicked her notion that she should start out *mean* and later move into *nice*. This was somewhat different from her ideas of caring and controlling at the beginning of the term. Caring and controlling now had conditions: how they were enacted depended on the sorts of student groups one faced. She was not ready to care by challenging the tracking system, but she was willing to experiment with various classroom groupings and curricular innovations in all her classes. Kerry had not shunted caring to a sidetrack. She was trying to reconcile the need to control individuals within a large group setting with her need to be liked and to care for students.

Daria

Daria had just turned 21 when I first interviewed her. She had grown up in a small, agriculturally based town and had attended a school that graduated 115 students. She was European-American.

Her mother worked in a textile factory, and her father was a poultry farmer. Daria's academic history was a common one in this heavily rural state. She had graduated near the top of her high school class, had scored moderately well on the SAT, and then had been admitted to a prestigious state university. There she quickly realized that she was not prepared to compete for good grades with many suburban, urban, and out-of-state students. Daria lived in an off-campus apartment with several friends during the senior year.

For Daria, being a teacher had not been a dream or a long-term desire.

> I floated around for awhile, and then decided on education. I thought about it, because it has all the negative stereotypes. But I like working with people, and I wanted to make a decision. So I worked at a camp. It was different than teaching, you were there 24 hours a day. I learned a lot through them [students]. I couldn't decide what age group to teach; I decided to teach middle grades when I observed last year [in an education course]. I saw a really good teacher. I'm from a really small town, and I didn't see that many good teachers. (11/17)

Her ideas of why she wished to teach were not clearly spelled out, except that she generally liked people and she had worked

with middle grades students. Daria recalled mainly negative
examples of teaching, unlike Kerry's primarily positive recollec-
tions of prior teachers.

Intending to Care

Daria described teaching as "playing." Not playing as "having
fun," but playing as acting. She highlighted the interplay
between "acting" and "being real."

> Daria: You have to have the ability [to teach well], but
>   you're on stage. On certain days, I'll have to act. On
>   certain days it would be real. You owe it to students
>   to *act*, when you may not feel like it. I had teachers
>   who didn't even want to be there. I did have an
>   incredible science teacher. In class he was himself,
>   real natural. I want to be approachable, be real.
>   (10/17)

She wanted to be herself, to be natural—her ideas of *self-
portrayal*. For Daria, caring entailed being real, and yet she felt
that teaching was akin to being on stage. She owed it to the
students to act as a responsible, approachable adult.

Daria also connected *curricular caring* with learning content
that was relevant. As with Kerry, she intended that students
learn "something that will help them when they're out of
school." She wanted to go beyond "entertainment" and "little
memorization test[s]" (11/28). When she observed a teacher
prior to student teaching, she wrote, "I'd call on them to give
answers instead of calling them all out myself. I don't think I'd
teach *to* a test. I'd also be interested in the novel they're reading.
I think it's relevant to their life" (2/9). But Daria was not sure
that she had acquired the necessary content in college to go
beyond a routine curriculum.

Daria seldom talked of *extracurricular caring* about students.
She did not recount stories of working with children in camp, as
had Kerry. When Daria provided details of caring for individual
students, it was nearly always in tandem with her thoughts on
controlling.

Possible Conflicts with Caring

It was stated earlier that Daria wanted to be herself while playing an adult role. She had some ideas about possible problems associated with that stance:

Daria:	I have a feel for the literary part of English. I watched a wonderful teacher who had children do plays; she was very creative.
Researcher:	Was she inspiring?
Daria:	Yeah, she had their respect and also motivated them. I want to be their friend, but you can't be buddy-buddy.
Researcher:	How do you do that?
Daria:	You try to be yourself and to stay in an adult role. You joke around but give off an authoritative presence. I worked at a camp, and I saw the difference between myself and the volunteers, who couldn't separate themselves from the kids. (10/17)

Daria wanted to care for children, to be a friend, without falling over some nebulous edge into the land of "buddy-buddy." She hoped that during class she could "lighten it up and play, and then get to business" (11/28). Daria set "being strong" and "being nice" as opposing actions. She was uncertain whether she could successfully balance the controlling and the caring. Daria's uncertainties centered on control over student behavior; she did not mention self-control. Thus, some obstacles loomed. Daria wanted not to be scared, though she was; she wanted to be decisive, though she believed she was not; and she wanted to be strong, though she perceived herself as perhaps being too nice.

Enacting Caring and Controlling

During student teaching, Daria's initial journal entries and comments in interviews portrayed her desire to care for students. Reflecting her tendency to view caring in broad terms, she said she had "gotten to know the kids better" (3/17), though she told few individual stories of *extracurricular caring*. Caring for

Daria, however, was primarily *curricular*. She wanted to let students be more active by "doing stuff" and "talking."

> Daria: I hate diagramming. She's done that for seven weeks. I mean she's [the cooperating teacher] still teaching it, you know? I was having to check diagramming. How much more boring can you get? Then I got to do poetry and it was like, "I can make this fun." Because when she mentioned it, they were like, "Ooh, yuck." I heard those moans and groans out there. "And I'm here to tell you that you're going to change your mind."
>
> Researcher: Good, good.
>
> Daria: . . . You know, I shouldn't be teaching English. (*Laughs*) It's no fun. And it's hard for me to make that fun, if I don't like it.(3/17)

Daria clearly equated teaching something she liked—and was confident about—with student response and "feeling like a teacher." Daria was in a tough position, one common to many student teachers. She was reluctant to question content because of the cooperating teacher's strongly held opinions about learning grammar in the classroom. Yet she wanted to teach something she liked and knew. The nature of public school curricula and the cooperating teacher's interpretations of the curriculum resulted in a misfit.

Curricular caring also meant helping students do well on the daily tasks of schooling, the worksheets and tests. She focused on individual students' learning difficulties. The following tale about Jeremy, one of the few individual stories, is illustrative of this intention to help them "get it right."

> Daria: Did I tell you about Jeremy? The first day I was in there and I was helping them do subjects, something on nouns. And he had all these things wrong, and he would come here to ask me to help him do one, but when I'd verbalize and say, "What is—okay, what's going on in this sentence?" He has to look at it and think about it . . . You know, I'm like, "Well, think about it, what's doing this?" And he's like,

> "Ohh . . ." The first day, we went over the home-
> work answers and he raised his hand to answer. It
> was the one I'd helped him with.

Researcher: Okay.

Daria: It was the *only* one that he got right. But then he
raised his hand because he wanted to participate
because he knew it. And that may be the only thing
he learned this week, but he knew that an interrogative sentence asked a question. Every time I ask
about it: "Who can tell me what an interrogative
sentence is?" (Puts her hand up in the air.)

Researcher: That's great. (3/17)

"Getting it right" was not meant to be merely a rote operation.
While there was little lengthy discussion of what students
should learn while they were having fun or being active, Daria
expressed strong opinions about the overemphasis on memorization of facts.

Daria struggled to take an adult role that required controlling.
She was quite uncertain of the effects of letting students talk.
Some of them were certainly actively behaving in ways that bothered Daria. Early on, she wrote benignly that students in 4th
period were "getting too active," but that she was "not annoyed"
(3/3). By the end of the second week, control was becoming a
problem in 4th period. Daria responded by issuing warnings and
reprimands, and developed a backup plan to put in place when
she finished the planned lesson early, and students tended to get
rowdy (3/6). She was devoting attention to "the row," a group of
boys in 4th period who gave her fits (3/17).

Daria described the initial struggle between "getting them
quiet" and "wanting them to like me"—between controlling
and being cared about. This resembled Kerry's concerns about
"being liked" and "being in control."

Daria: I feel the struggle between wanting them to like me.
Because they don't really like her [the cooperating
teacher]. Because she's so strict on discipline, she
likes them quiet and everything. . . . I mean I want
them to work if I want them to work, but at the end

of the class and they kind of have a little free time and they're packing up, I don't care that much. And then we have this assistant principal out in the hall or something, and I'm like "Oh, I'd better have them quiet." So I feel a struggle between that and wanting them to like me. Because the other day when I started the poetry, those kids liked me then, they responded. But they respected me too, because it was like a little bit different. I don't know, it was a neat feeling. . . .

Daria repeated her intention that the students have fun and that she be liked. But problems of control kept cropping up, and the students failed to respond as she wished.

Researcher: Are you ready to teach? Do you feel like teaching now?

Daria: I don't know. Today in 6th period I had a horrible time, though I don't think they're as bad with me as they are with her. I don't know if they feel sorry for me or they have sympathy or they like me better, but I mean, they just give her—they cause extra problems for me, but maybe it just doesn't bother me. I don't get annoyed as bad as she does. (3/10)

She did not want to "just punish everybody else" for the transgressions of a few (3/17). But the problems of control began to take precedence over all else. Daria had started student teaching with a positive though vague idea of enacting caring. A second phase now began, where she simply tried to avoid the negative. She did not want to "dread the class," and worried about embarrassing students if she should get "too mean." She feared asserting control and possibly "becoming the enemy" (4/7).

In her efforts to get students active and to help students get it right, Daria wanted to do group work in the classroom. But she foresaw a problem from two directions: the students might have been so used to the cooperating teacher that they would oppose anything different; and the cooperating teacher was hesitant about the group activities, because they might adversely affect classroom control.

The group activities Daria attempted did not significantly change student behavior. There was much student chatter and movement in class, especially 4th period. Daria wanted to link caring for individuals—getting on a personal level in class—with controlling in the classroom. She was seeking the complementarity of caring and controlling. But as she felt more out of control in the classroom, particularly in 4th period, that complementarity appeared illusory.

She became more concerned with matters of self-control than with *self-portrayal*. Daria deemed herself "indecisive," and the pace of classroom interactions proved problematic for her. She felt there was a dilemma with being herself and also acting as an adult teacher who was assertively in charge.

By the second week in April, matters came to a head. Daria had moved students, had called them down in class numerous times, "had a little chat," had used "the warning," and had put names on the board many times (4/3, 4/4, 4/9, 4/13). Some of the students were "jerks"; she felt "exhausted." An incident with one boy triggered an emotional scene, both in school and for days afterward. Things were out of control for Daria.

Daria:	You haven't heard my worst experience. It's lucky you didn't talk to me last Friday.
Researcher:	What happened?
Daria:	Let's see, for the first time I put them in groups to work, and they couldn't handle it. They were all over the place.
Researcher:	Fourth period?
Daria:	Yeah. And I gave them marks too [on the board]. It was frustrating me even stronger than today, if that's possible, and both of them had detention hall, already, on the board, and Sean has the audacity to walk up to the board and erase his name, so he got a fourth check. He didn't understand why he should stay in the classroom. And then he started to walk out. And I guess he walked by me on his way and I reached out and took his arm right there and held it

and I said, "Sean, go back to your seat." And he went, "No," and I said, "Back to your seat." And he went back and sat down. But after class, he ignored me, and went to the principal's office and said that I hit him in class.

Researcher: So, did the principal call you in?

Daria: I talked to _____ [the assistant principal].

Researcher: What did she say to you?

Daria: She just wanted to hear my side. She'd already pretty much taken care of it. (4/12)

Caring and controlling were now at odds. The incident with Sean appeared to put Daria at the edge—of her patience and her feelings of caring with which she had entered. Daria originally thought the conflict revolved around being a "friend" versus being "buddy-buddy," but by the end of student teaching she had amended that: she was now concerned with being personal with students, but not with being their friend. Daria asserted that she would trade being liked for being in control. Daria attributed her troubles to her approach toward "classroom management." As a remedy, she attended a weekend workshop that offered some different perspectives on methods of controlling. Daria believed that she should adopt a discipline system that incorporated "quality attention"—a positive incentive for students—in addition to the negative consequences of "assertive discipline." For the next two weeks she gave detentions (4/19), sent students to in-school suspension (4/26), and tried to be consistent in the methods of controlling. Though she did not institute a positive system of responding to difficult students, she kept her emotions under control and somehow managed to maintain a positive demeanor until the end.

Jackie

Jackie was 22 and had grown up in unusual circumstances for a student at this university. Jackie was African-American. She had attended school for a time in New York City, while living at home with her mother and brothers. Sometime in the middle grades she had become a foster care child, and had moved to a rural area of North Carolina to live with a minister's family. Her high school graduating class included 202 students.

Though Jackie got a low score on the SAT, she was admitted to the university on a probationary status. For much of her college career she teetered just on the edge of academic probation or dismissal. During the fall semester of 1988, Jackie had to attain a certain GPA in order to student teach the next spring. She attributed her ability to undergo academic and social difficulties to her faith in God: "What had kept me from going under is that I'm saved. . . . I still have tests and trials; that doesn't change" (10/14).

Jackie had come to college wanting to be a nurse but then had changed her mind: "My girlfriends told me the truth about nursing. The terrible hours, having to work holidays. I wanted something much more flexible, where the hours are better. Teaching was always a second choice" (10/18).

Intending to Care

Jackie carried strong images of teachers. She could recall "their voices, what they wear," and she wanted to "follow in their footsteps. . . . My teacher had an accent—I can't put my finger on it—very wise, in her subject and in life" (10/31). She wanted to care as a person, and as a teacher. One of Jackie's college teachers had encouraged her to "be yourself."

> Dr. U. taught me how to play many roles and not just narrow ones. He taught me to be really open and to be myself and not be afraid of who I am and what I stand for. Don't feel offended or intimidated; be yourself. (11/3)

She took the advice to heart. Jackie pictured herself modeling honesty and adult stability for her students. In addition to being a role model, a good teacher would be open and would talk with students outside of class, exhibiting *extracurricular caring*. Jackie held that teachers had a long-term responsibility for students, one which went beyond classroom boundaries.

I don't want to just limit myself to be a professor. I want to have an influence on students' lives outside the classroom. I got a lot of information about life from my teachers. Students should not just be on their "p's and q's" in my classroom. The class should help them in the long run . . . Some students put on a front. I want them to be real, to perform to their abilities, not just in my classroom. (11/2)

The intimation here was that she did not merely want to control students so they would stay on their "p's and q's." Extracurricular caring meant helping them to be "real" in their interactions with other people.

In the short-term situation of a class session, Jackie felt responsible for having students "get the material." A teacher was supposed to maintain expectations for student learning.

If I give the kids a test and they don't do well, I should think about myself. Maybe the material was too hard or they didn't study. When I'm getting the material across, testing is not the only way. Calling on students, reviewing, doing those things you can tell if you have been successful. (11/2)

Curricular caring thus entailed testing students only on material covered in class and grading their work fairly. Notice that there was no mention of the content of one's instruction. This differed from Kerry, who conceived of activities and the relevancy of the content as crucial to her ideas of caring. Daria, too, had spoken of relevant information.

Jackie also wanted to act informally at times. With one high school teacher she had "felt like I was in prison" (10/31). She believed that all good teachers were "laid back, not too structured."

Jackie: The teachers [in high school] weren't so structured. We should have a casual side, too. My 12th grade teacher was so tense, I couldn't think . . . In the good classes you could ask questions. I wasn't afraid to raise my hand. . . . My English 1 and 2 teachers were incredible; they were casual and prepared. In

> English 1 we could bring in any literature we wanted
> and expand on it. (10/18)

It was a combination of being "casual" and "prepared"—
enacting self-portrayal and curricular caring—that Jackie
sought.

Possible Conflicts with Caring

Jackie wanted to be an adult authority in control of the
classroom at the same time that she intended to care for students.
When asked "What are some of the difficulties of teaching?"
Jackie replied:

Jackie: Being accepted, by co-workers and students, for my
            performance as a teacher. I want to have an impact.
            I want them [students] to feel free to come by my
            room and yet maintain that professional side. And
            still maintain a personal relationship. . . . That has
            some risk to it. Some students might take advantage
            of it. (10/31)

During her college career Jackie had felt controlled by the
academic environment (the classroom expectations, the grading
scheme). As a teacher, she intended to be in control of the
environment and the curriculum, which might result in conflicts
with her desires to care for students.

Enacting Caring and Controlling

Jackie had no problems controlling her emotions in the classroom. She seemed not to follow Kerry's pattern of letting things
that bothered her slide, until she got angry or had to act *mean*.
Instead of going from *nice* to *mean* as Kerry believed that she had
done, Jackie's form of *self-portrayal* was to express personal and
professional authority from the start.

Before student teaching Jackie had stated that teachers cared
about students by "being themselves." In practice, however,
that form of personal caring was constantly threatened.
Throughout student teaching she felt stymied by others' expec-

tations of her—the cooperating teacher, the students, the university supervisor. Jackie originally appraised herself as weak in subject matter, so it was no surprise that her problems of control included uncertainties about whether she could handle the "AG" classes full of academic achievers. Controlling would in part require that she portray herself as an authority in the subject (Social Studies). She wrote:

> I want to be myself in my teaching but I have discovered I'm only myself during 2nd, 3rd, and 4th academic, and when my cooperative teacher is not in the room. I appreciate all that my cooperative teacher does for me, because she does a lot. She answers my questions. She helps me with my lesson plans. She helps me find resources and activities for the kids. But all that is irrelevant if she does not let me be me in the classroom. (3/29)

Self-portrayal had to do with making the decisions, and, in personal terms, determining how to control and to care. "Being me" was not related to creating activities that diverged from the cooperating teacher's methods or to bringing in unusual content. She struggled with "being herself" and "being casual" while she was trying to carry out the lesson plan and to appear knowledgeable.

Jackie had intended to be "personal" and yet "professional." She enacted *extracurricular caring* by being physically affectionate with students, in a manner similar to Kerry's. When she and I were walking down the hall after lunch, Jackie pointed out another student and said "That's my girl." Pointing to a nearby male student she told me "He's one of my boys" (3/30). She would put her arms around students, hug them, ask them about how things were going outside of school.

Jackie established an almost familial feeling for some of the students. She tried to use her knowledge of "her kids" to ensure that they behaved appropriately. She recognized the possible problems with extracurricular caring: that it might lead to favoritism or problems of control in class. There were situations where Jackie felt the tug between individual caring and maintaining her authority as an adult, and she believed that in this circumstance (student teaching) she had to choose control over caring. She felt often that she had to act her part as an "authority" by following "procedures" and projecting a very firm tone and demeanor.

Jackie's personal affection for students was in several cases coupled with an effort to help a student academically outside of regular class time. This journal entry about Nakia indicated how Jackie acted to care for individuals.

> Although there is so much involved in teaching, I'm glad I decided to get into the field. I really like it a lot. Of course, by now I have established bonds with some of the students, particularly Ben, Marcus, Nakia, Kim, etc. . . . I'm still giving Nakia special academic assistance, because I don't want her to flunk the 7th grade. I do care enough about her situation to give some special attention to it. It's not easy on me at times, but I'm determined to help her. (3/30)

So Jackie tutored students, before and during her student teaching. That was her form of *curricular caring*. Jackie wanted to help the students having the most difficulty. She felt closer to the "basic" students than to the "gifted" students.

> Researcher: You've told me on several occasions that you have a real place in your heart for some of the slower kids.
>
> Jackie: And I try to remember; I always remind myself that they really need one-on-one help. (4/4)

Jackie spent time tutoring Joseph, a student needing special help. She wrote:

> I had to help Joseph again on his test. . . . He can barely read. But I felt real good about helping Joseph this time. . . . I really like Joseph, because in spite of his learning disability he tries very hard. And, given some individual attention Joseph does very well. He ACED the test. (3/1; *emphasis in original*)

Jackie's comments on caring for a group were personal; they involved her social relationships with some individuals in the group. She occasionally talked about the relevance of the activities or the content, though she did not articulate her social goals for the classes. Here was a point at which Jackie considered curricular caring in group terms.

> Researcher: What about the fables did you think helped the story move along?
>
> Jackie: Something in which the student can relate to, something in the fable or the traditional fables are switched around animals, but then we have our own personal fables, too. We have experiences that occur in our lives, and we learn from them. We learn some kind of moral lesson. That's why I like the students to kind of give me some of their personal experiences.
>
> Researcher: I thought that was real clever. Was that something that you thought of, or did you get the idea—
>
> Jackie: Um, actually in the last seminar. So I was doing some background reading on India, and fables were a major part of the Indian culture. I thought it was good. (4/11)

Jackie sometimes attempted to respond to students' questions about the meaning of the curriculum. On one occasion a student had asked how historians knew about what the textbooks claimed was true.

> Researcher: She said: "Well, how do we know that they were the first people?"
>
> Jackie: Oh, I went on to tell her that historians researched, and they had left records. You know, that was the best answer I had.
>
> Researcher: What kinds of alternative answers do you think there are for that question about why we—for either question, "How do we know that?" or "Why do we need to know that?" Because it kind of follows one upon the other.
>
> Jackie: Historians research and they find the information. They publish and teachers teach it. I try to show them how it all fits together. It's almost like moving from elementary to high school to college, you know . . . I study to learn. I study so that I can pass. I learn so I can, you know, whatever it means. (4/11)

Jackie wanted to "make it all fit together" for her students, yet she saw teachers as implementers of a given curriculum. She worked straightforwardly through the textbook and did not question the course content. Her activities involved primarily whole-group activities or seatwork and rarely small groups, which are more difficult to control. The questioning techniques alternated between flexibility and tight control. At times, she would ask probing questions or follow up a student's question by elaborating on the issue; at other points she would ask questions but not delve into the subject matter. This is not in itself unusual for a teacher to do. What Jackie did, especially with the "gifted" students in 1st period, was to control the content of the questions so that most questions were factual and therefore would not lead her into foreign territory that might be unfamiliar. She appeared to control the curriculum in order to control classroom events.

So Jackie did not have the plethora of concerns and uncertainties about control as Kerry and Daria did. Her problem was to know when to deviate from the plan, because her inclination was to "make it through." She did not want to be controlled by others, and yet felt that she could not change the system of student teaching. She came to distrust her cooperating teacher, whose interruptions and constant presence prevented her from being the sort of teacher she had imagined. In spite of all this, as we shall see, she wanted to believe that caring and controlling were connected.

THE COMPLEMENTARITY OF CARING AND CONTROLLING

The Limits of Caring

All three participants—Kerry, Jackie, and Daria—intended to care and control and expressed the sense of conflict that Caruso (1977), Tardif (1985), and Walberg (1968) described. Caring was repeatedly limited by the need to control.

According to all three student teachers' initial ethics of care, one should present oneself honestly and openly to others. The three participants, prior to student teaching, intended to "be

real" (Kerry), to "be myself" (Jackie), to "be natural" (Daria).
Each of the three found this aspect of caring—*self-portrayal*—to
be quite difficult in the daily press of student teaching.

Daria was confused about how to portray herself. She talked of
"leaving dreamland," and part of that notion was that she could
not be natural in the classroom, she could not be herself as she
had imagined while dreaming in college classrooms. Jackie was
not able to be herself because she did not feel in control. First,
the classroom really belonged to the cooperating teacher. And
some of the students made it difficult to be oneself. Jackie
marked off limits to the trust she could place in students'
responses to her words and actions. She portrayed herself to a
select group of students and classes. Kerry fought hard not to
seem *mean* when she meant to be *nice*. Spontaneity gave way in
part to planning for more complex group interactions and to
more structured attempts to control misbehavior.

The participants also expected to give personal affection to
others and to be cared for in return. Jackie and Kerry wanted to
know students outside of class and even school hours. Daria
mentioned "'liking people" as one reason for choosing to teach,
though she did not elaborate on the nature of personal caring for
individual students. These *extracurricular* relationships with
students were perceived as possibly being helpful when dealing
with issues of control in the classroom. But one had to be wary
of letting extracurricular relationships interfere with the need for
fairness and control. Kerry's discussion of her project to "save"
Kevin was indicative of a further understanding about the temporal and structural limits of caring. After doing personal things,
such as cleaning out his locker, Kerry reconsidered her initial
approach:

| University Supervisor: | Is there a problem in your master plan to change Kevin's approach to class? |
| Kerry: | Yes, in fact I feel different this week than last. I'm backing away a bit from my master plan. I don't think in my short time here that I'll really reform Kevin. If I could just get him to write down assign- ments and bring his books to class, I'd be happy.(3/23) |

Kerry in this brief account described one of the constraining conditions of student teaching: it is short term. Caring in this context—student teaching—inevitably has its limits. "Master plans" that look to reform a student's patterns of behavior are often extracurricular and long term and are not suited to the temporal conditions of student teaching. Kerry scaled down her expectations because there simply was not enough time to care for everyone, and student teachers had to live up to their supervisors' expectations.

The matter of the limits of *curricular caring* requires a bit of explanation. According to Berman (1987), teachers and students should be engaged in a shared construction of knowledge. When a teacher chooses to facilitate a process whereby students make meaning from what they are studying—when knowledge is perceived as being co-generated in classrooms—this constitutes an act of caring. The process of curricular caring can be enacted with individuals during a lesson or during nonclass hours. According to this conception, the prerequisite for caring is a teacher's openness to learning from students, and a willingness to explore mutually the topics under discussion.

This theoretical curricular caring is difficult to enact in the classroom. McNeil (1988) found a connection between the role ambiguities of teaching and teachers' tendencies to control curriculum. On an individual level, teachers wanted to control students because of uncertainties about their own content knowledge and about the consequences of student behavior. On a social level, there were tensions between an ill-defined and fluid professional role and the constraints of the school environment. Without support for their professional authority, teachers created their own authority by controlling the curriculum and especially the content, which enabled them to better control the students' behavior. This was seen by McNeil as a choice of *social control* over *educational goals*. The teachers controlled course content by omitting controversial issues, omitting content requiring in-depth treatment, rarely asking students to add their ideas to the lesson, and reducing complicated topics to lists of terms and facts. McNeil labeled this a "defensive teaching strategy," designed to get one through under control without asking too much of students.

This sort of defensive strategy may well result from conflicts of caring and controlling. For the student teachers, curricular caring encompassed the relevancy and scope of the content and the challenge of the classroom activities which they utilized. At times, both Daria and Jackie controlled the content of their classes, soliciting few questions from students and tightly circumscribing the kinds of questions they asked of students. Daria was initially concerned with the relevancy of content and the motivation of the activities, but she eventually chose not to challenge the cooperating teacher's system. Jackie mentioned "getting the material across," but rarely questioned the relevancy or value of the content. To some extent the two student teachers' handling of content conflicted with several aspects of caring: to engage students in considering complex issues and to include their ideas and experiences in the shaping of the curriculum. There was little "shared construction of knowledge."

Kerry, like Daria, wanted the content to be relevant to students' lives. She wanted students to learn how to study and to think for themselves. Kerry also spoke directly about "learning from the students," and her idea of a reciprocal relationship may have been analogous to Berman's ideas about a "shared construction of knowledge." So the three participants entered student teaching with some conception of curricular caring, though it did not precisely match the ideals of Noddings, Berman, and others who would have teachers seriously challenge the content and processes of curriculum.

Within Noddings's theoretical ethic of care, one can also promote caring by asking, "What effect will my actions have on the creation of a caring community?" (Noddings, 1986). I have not heretofore discussed this aspect of *communal caring*, because the three participants in my study did not talk about "community" prior to student teaching. Kerry did evidence an interest in communal caring when she described her experiences as a summer camp counselor. During student teaching Kerry experimented with various groupings of students and commented to students and supervisors about establishing the right social atmosphere in her classes. Her social and curricular goals were deemed important, though her understanding of how and why to create community were not well developed.

Jackie was leery of small groups and did not set social goals of caring that entailed teacher actions in the classroom. A sense of caring in a group was developed outside of class with "her kids" and in our conversations, more than in classroom interactions.

Daria spoke directly about her fears of engaging students in small group work. One way to create a community of caring is to allow students to work together, to learn from each other in smaller settings. And it is generally more difficult to maintain control over every student's behavior in those circumstances. Daria and her cooperating teacher did not try such arrangements because of the possibility of misbehavior—the loss of control.

Connections between Caring and Controlling

Before student teaching, the participants in my study had sometimes conceived of teaching problems as polar positions, between which there was only one good choice (Kerry's "being real vs. being intellectual"). But the participants' words also showed that they wished not to stand near the poles, but rather to assume a position where they could keep sight of seemingly conflicting aims. In the words of the participants in my study, they wanted to be both a person and a teacher. They wanted personal and institutional relationships as the basis for their authority. Problems arose in part from their beliefs that they must choose between the two. Their final summaries showed that they had not given up on connecting caring and controlling.

In the final personal interview Kerry expressed sadness at the thought of leaving—this only six days after her "wash-my-hands-of-it" speech that exhibited real anger and frustration about her lack of control in 5th period. Kerry had begun student teaching by talking about the reciprocity of caring and self-control:

> Kerry: I think they sense my basis for the way I try to act is, if I can prove to them that I'm human, that I'll respect them if they respect me, and if there's that

> ongoing thing, then we're fine. And we can joke, we
> can play. But when it's time to quit, we both quit.
> (3/17)

In the end Kerry still wanted mutual respect and mutual restraint (self-control) on everyone's part. While she intended to maintain her spontaneity, she thought she ought not be "winging it," a sentiment perhaps relating to curricular caring. There were remaining uncertainties about how to care in a (positively) controlled way, but she vowed that she would not "become cynical" (5/9). She wanted to connect caring and controlling in her own way.

Just as Kerry had done, in the end Daria averred that teachers should "deal with [students] as a person." The limits were there: one could not be "friends," but it helped to be "personal" (5/5). She wrote that she was "really sick" of two students because "they just don't care" (4/26). Yet she was unwilling to direct her negative feelings toward other students. She worried that she had "shortchanged the other students in 4th period." "I think they know I care, but I'm not sure they've learned a whole heck of a lot! That scares me" (4/26). Daria saw the importance of curricular caring and recognized the need for a limited, responsive control during classroom interactions. She had wanted to connect caring and controlling in some way. Though she did not fully characterize student teaching as a success, she had "survived it" and now aimed to "become more confident."

Jackie intended to "be personal" and also "be professional." Although her desire to control was alluded to earlier in this chapter, Jackie was certainly not altogether sure of herself in the classroom. "My students at times are too live. I don't feel like I'm losing control of the classes. I just feel like I've got to find that midpoint where I am fair, but assertive and firm" (4/11). Fairness was an outgrowth of caring, and authority had to be both personal and professional. She had not seriously acted on connecting curricular caring and control, but she wanted to keep hold of the extracurricular caring regardless of her need to be a controlling authority. She retained images of how school might be, visions from high school. Her eloquent phrases about the power and difficulties of love need not be further amplified.

Jackie: In my high school we were family . . .

Researcher: That's a strong word, *family*.

Jackie: I picture the sharing times. If your dad's out of work, people help you. They are supportive, caring, and sharing. The three together is *love*. That means also not being inconsiderate.

Researcher: How do you get "family"?

Jackie: You've gotta grow into it. In a natural family you do, too. It's a growing process, you've got to win their love. . . . [In a classroom] you have to *show* it. But you've got to be careful; people don't always know what you mean. (5/8)

Personal Caring/Professional Caring

In summary, I believe first that it is simplistic to assume that personal caring is opposed to or separate from professional caring. Caring and controlling are parts of a whole identity as teacher, not one role among many. If ethical caring is to be enacted, the teacher is always a person portraying herself or himself, while a role represents the interactions between individual intentions and interpretations of institutional expectations. Being a teacher requires both *authenticity* (portraying oneself honestly) and *legitimacy* ("functioning as part of a 'moral community' with norms of collegiality and experimentation") (Buchmann, 1986, p. 65). In my study, narratives of caring as self and teacher were intermixed; *self-portrayal*, and *extra curricular* and *curricular caring*, were all evident at points.

Secondly, the finding of conflict between caring and controlling does not signal their necessary juxtaposition. Ethical caring requires boundaries on self-portrayal, on the establishment of personal relationships through extracurricular caring, on the dialogue with students that represents curricular caring, and on the creation of community.

Ethical caring demands self-control. Being oneself is not the aim of teaching, and we need not elevate "person" over "teacher," or predilection over principle. Buchmann (1986) points out the weakness of teachers relying solely on their "personal reasons" when analyzing what occurred in the classroom.

Caring ethically as a person is not synonomous with tossing out myopic rationales. The teacher must be controlled enough not to allow emotional difficulties, or extracurricular relationships with some students, or a reliance on spontaneity to interfere with students' opportunity to learn.

Ethical caring also requires some control over the environment, and does not allow certain students to dominate classroom interactions. Empowering others includes helping them to set limits, and establishing a good classroom environment. A student teacher, as all teachers, controls content and student behavior to some degree. Part of caring entails controlling group interactions to the extent that positive social interactions can occur.

On the other hand, control without personal caring can close off doorways to an understanding of a student's motivations for learning or not learning and to student-generated questions or ideas which challenge the givens of textbook and teacher-talk. Controlling clearly has its limits. In my study, Daria maintained her desire to care, as evidenced by her analysis of the limitations of the assertive discipline system she had enacted. She was, in the end, unwilling to forsake caring for controlling.

Perhaps most germane to the issue of possible complementarity, both caring and controlling may be conceived of as examples of "social connection" and not necessarily "independent social competence" (Eaker & Paul, 1988). Student teachers certainly want ethical caring and some form of control that will enable them to fulfill their expectations of capably holding a professional, adult role. At its core, teaching involves establishing a professional relationship with learners. A professional relationship is marked by ethical caring and controlling.

Learning to be a teacher does not require a transformation from *person* to *teacher*, but a faithful effort to be both person and teacher. All three participants entered student teaching with desires to care. They hoped to portray themselves openly to students, to establish reciprocal relationships, to confirm the students, and, in some vague form, to promote a community. The conflicts of caring and controlling seemed to overwhelm them on numerous occasions, and the enacting of caring in that context became quite problematic. Yet they held fast to their notions that they could be both person and teacher. Their voices should not go unheard in the din of cries for "professionalism." Professionalism should encompass a commitment to ethical caring and an understanding of the conflicts and complementarity of caring and controlling.

REFERENCES

Berman, L.M. (1987). The teacher as decision maker. In F.S. Bolin & J.M. Falk (Eds.), Teacher renewal. New York Teachers College Press.

Buchmann, M. (1986). Role over person: Legitimacy and authenticity in teaching. In M. Ben-Peretz, R. Bromme, & R. Halkes (Eds.), Advances of research on teacher thinking. Berwyn: Swets North America.

Buchmann, M. (1989, April). Breaking from experience in teacher education: When is it necessary, how is it possible? Paper presented at Annual Meeting of the American Educational Research Association, San Francisco.

Caruso, J.J. (1977). Phases in student teaching. Young children, 33, 57–63.

Cole, M. (1985). The tender trap? Commitment and consciousness in entrants to teaching. In P.T. Ashton & R.D. Webb (Eds.), Making a difference: Teachers' sense of efficacy and student achievement. New York: Longman.

Eaker, D.J., & Paul, J.L. (1988, February). The meaning of caring for education. Paper presented at the Ethnography in Education Forum, Philadelphia.

Fuller, F. (1969). Concerns of teachers: A developmental characterization. American Educational Research Journal, 6, 207–226.

Gaskell, P.J. (1975). Patterns and changes in the perspectives of student teachers: A participant observation study. Unpublished dissertation, Harvard University, Cambridge, MA.

Gibson, G. (1976). The effects of school practice: The development of student perspectives. British Journal of Teacher Education, 2, 241–250.

Goodman, J. (1985). Field-based experience: A study of social control and student teachers' response to institutional constraints. Journal of Education for Teaching, 11(1), 26–49.

Goodman, J. (1988). Constructing a practical philosophy of teaching: A study of preservice teachers' professional perspectives. Teaching and Teacher Education, 4 (2), 121–137.

Hoy, W. (1969). Pupil ideology and organization socialization: A further examination of the influence of experience on the beginning teacher. School Review, 77, 257–265.

Hoy, W., & Rees, R. (1977). The bureaucratic socialization of student teachers. Journal of Teacher Education, 28 (1), 23–26.

Iannaccone, L. (1963). Student teaching: A traditional stage in the making of a teacher. Theory into Practice, 2, 73–80.

Kleinsasser, A.M. (1989, March). *Four facets of classroom ownership emerging from a grounded theory of novice language arts teachers' knowledge of practice.* Paper presented at Annual Meeting of the American Educational Research Association, San Francisco.

Linkous, V. (1989). *Patterns of caring: A study of the perceptions of teachers and students.* Unpublished dissertation, Virginia Polytechnic University.

Liston, D.P., & Zeichner, K.M. (1987). Reflective teacher education and moral deliberation. *Journal of Teacher Education, 38* (6), 2–8.

McNeil, L. (1988). *Contradictions of control.* New York: Routledge.

Moon, R.A., Niemeyer, R.C., & Karls, E.A. (1989, March). *The language of transformation: An examination of the student teacher's process of transformation of experience to personal knowledge.* Paper presented at Annual Meeting of the American Educational Research Association, San Francisco.

Noddings, N. (1984). *Caring: A feminine approach to ethics and moral education.* Berkeley, CA: University of California Press.

Noddings, N. (1986). Fidelity in teaching, teacher education, and research for teaching. *Harvard Educational Review, 56,* 496–510.

Petty, M., & Hogben, D. (1980). Explorations of semantic space with beginning teachers: A study of socialization into teaching. *British Journal of Teacher Education, 6,* 51–61.

Popkewitz, T.S., Tabachnick, B.R., & Zeichner, K.M. (1979). Dulling the senses: Research in teacher education. *Journal of Teacher Education, 30*(5), 52–60.

Prillaman, R. (1988). *The acquisition of role identities of teachers.* Unpublished dissertation, University of North Carolina-Chapel Hill.

Sitter, J.P. (1982). *The student teaching experience from the perspective of the student teacher: A descriptive study.* Unpublished dissertation, Michigan State University.

Tabachnick, B.R., & Zeichner, K.M. (1984). The impact of the student teaching experience on the development of teacher perspectives. *Journal of Teacher Education, 35*(6), 28–36.

Tardif, C. (1985). On becoming a teacher: The student teacher's perspective. *The Alberta Journal of Educational Research, 31*(2), 139–148.

Tom, A.R. (1985). Inquiring into inquiry-oriented teacher education. *Journal of Teacher Education, 36*(6), 35–44.

Walberg, H. (1968). Personality-role conflict and self-conception in urban practice teaching. *School Review, 76,* 41–48.

Part IV

Caring From The Ivory Tower: Experiences Of Researchers And Professors

Chapter 7

Researcher Relationships and Responsibilities: Consider with Care*

Jaci Webb

Imagine that, once upon a time, the "Ten Commandments of Field Research" were handed down from on high. Inscribed on a sacred stone tablet and entrusted to an exotic people in some remote and isolated land, these commandments might someday be discovered by an enterprising ethnographer. There are those who believe that such a discovery could settle once and for all the controversy surrounding an ethic of research methodology, that we would then have The Word to use as our guide as we negotiate access and location and attempt to honor our responsibilities both to our participants and to our work itself. I would venture that the first of those commandments would read: "Honor thy subjects and their context; do not intrude," while the second would be a succinct and direct: "Get thee close."

I have defined myself and the work I do somewhere between these two putative "commandments"; and it seems increasingly clear to me that, for many researchers, these may become conflicting ethical considerations. Debates around "going native" vs. retaining an "objective gaze," about "getting close" and yet not "intruding," are perennial and ongoing. Such debates occur, not only professionally among researchers as they

*This work was supported by a grant from the Lilly Endowment Program on Youth and Caring

attempt to define the limits of their public role, but also at the personal level, as researchers journey into the field to confront their particular subjects within their chosen context, and as they attempt individual location in relationship to that confrontation.

My inclusion of both of these commandments—seemingly diametrically opposed to one another—in my tenets of field researcher methodology is meant to make salient my belief that the resulting professional debate is necessary. I don't begin to presume that I, or any researcher for that matter, can—or even should—attempt to resolve that tension: that ongoing contention is vital to keeping our work honest and meaningful. What I do propose is to try to open up this debate—that is, the one concerning the more personal, internal conflict. By so doing, I intend to examine the considerations that we undertake when we situate ourselves somewhere between those two positions, locating ourselves in the context of a study, in relationship with our participants, and in relation to the focus we have chosen to study. In the context of the study this work comes from, in relation to my participants, and with respect to the focus of the study—caring—these considerations have included what I have chosen to call *communion, testifying, witnessing, grace,* and finally, *self-knowledge.*

The study that provides the context for my discussion of these considerations is one in which four fellow researchers and I have been examining the nature of caring relationships in classrooms. The subjects are my colleagues on the Caring Study team. Beyond a general discussion of the researcher role, I intend to make a connection between this issue of location and the focus of the team's fieldwork, the issue of caring. In fact, I contend that a closer examination of the nature of the caring relationships that each researcher has—or, perhaps, has not—entered into in the classrooms where he or she has observed will prove to be most revealing in terms of how each of us has come to define our role as researcher and how we have set the limits of responsibility associated with those relationships. Those limits should further be revealed in a discussion of how each researcher has come to define caring as a result of what he or she has learned while in the field.

In a study that purports to look specifically at caring relationships between teachers and students and among students themselves, the inevitable tendency of the researcher is to want to become involved; movement away from the location of the totally objective and uninvolved onlooker may be greatly enhanced. Evidence of the need of students to make caring connections with available adults—in this case, researchers in their classrooms—may bring those researchers face to face with a dilemma of their own: How far into such relationships can, or should, researchers go? The inhibiting factors in this situation may extend well beyond that of the standard problem of the possible effects of observer intrusion on the collection and interpretation of data, to the deeper question of the responsibility that the establishment of a caring relationship inevitably brings.

Entering into relationships in the classroom, establishing social contracts with participants that carry with them subtle, and perhaps unintended, messages about duration and separation is a risky business. Consideration of the fine print of these covert clauses requires us to examine issues that are often obscured by superficial, even artificial, reflections upon "the basic corollary of participant observation" that exists in the assumption that the "role of the participant observer requires both detachment and personal involvement" (Patton, 1990, p. 191).

As I began to examine the issues framing this discussion, I chanced upon Carol Gilligan's (1982) study *In A Different Voice*, a book that seemed to echo the dialogue that had already begun to sound itself out in my mind. Gilligan tells the story of Ruth, a young woman who faces a decision that seems to place her squarely between what she perceives to be competing ethical images of herself: on the one hand, justice; on the other, "caring." Gilligan relates that, as Ruth agonizes over her decision (having to do with an unplanned pregnancy), she "describes herself as "going in two directions" and values that part of herself which is "incredibly passionate and sensitive," her "capacity to recognize and meet the needs of others":

> Because Ruth sees the acquisition of adult power as entailing the
> loss of feminine sensitivity and compassion, she construes the

conflict between femininity and adulthood as a moral problem. The abortion dilemma then directs her attention to what it means in this society to be a woman and to be an adult, and the recognition of the disparity between power and care initiates the search for a resolution that can encompass both femininity and adulthood, in relationships and at work. (Gilligan, 1982, pp. 97-98)

While Ruth's dramatic dilemma is—at first—seemingly far removed from our quiet narrative of researchers making judgements about the nature of their roles in an educational setting, consistent underlying themes in both center around conflicting ethics and competing images of responsibility. On their journeys into the field, researchers inevitably carry with them the same basic considerations, Gilligan's "fundamental images" of both justice and care. These ethical images are framed by other images of responsibility, adulthood, and professionalism. These images appear, in some contexts, to be both dichotomous and competing, and this duality creates a continuous tension that requires constant negotiation; in much the same way the tension created by the ongoing contention between our two commandments of location also require considerable consideration.

I have come to believe that this consideration must be contextual and grounded in the realities of the setting and the participants. And, while involvement in relationships in classrooms with children requires special consideration, owing more to the vulnerable and dependent nature of children, the dynamics of the negotiated relationship between the two adults in the setting, the teacher and the researcher, must also be taken in serious account. In this study in particular, therefore, an examination of the contexts of caring associated with the researchers themselves is most appropriate.

METHODOLOGY

As noted above, this particular study is a subcomponent of a larger one, the Caring Study, which was completed under a grant from the Lilly Endowment as part of their Research Grants

Program on Youth and Caring from 1989 through 1991. The focus of the umbrella study was the formation of caring relationships in classrooms and how they subsequently affect student attachment to school. The study was done in an urban elementary school in the Southeast, which served a student population drawn from two distinct communities, one consisting of mainly middle to upper lower income white families and the other of mostly lower income African-American families. Two members of the research team were in and out of the school for some four years, having entered with another project, which culminated in a written history of both the school and of the two parent communities that had combined their student populations during desegregation (in the early 70s) to form the core of the current school population. These two researchers reentered the school in the fall of 1989 to spend the school year doing classroom ethnographies in their designated classrooms. One, John, was a university professor with no public school teaching experience. He observed with Pam, an African-American second-grade teacher with 20-plus years of teaching experience. John was also the Principal Investigator directing the overall Caring Study. The other original researcher, Dean, was a graduate student with teaching experience in both public secondary schools and the university setting. His observations were done with Sally, a white fifth-grade teacher with nearly 20 years of teaching experience—all of it in the study site school.

The final two members of the team, not including myself, also entered the school during the fall of 1989 to conduct classroom ethnographies. One of these researchers, Wayne, had experience as both a public elementary school teacher and a university professor, while the other, Eve, had had experience as both a special educator working with children in kindergarten through high school and as a university instructor. Wayne spent a school year observing in the classroom of Martha, a white fourth-grade teacher with over 15 years of experience in the classroom—ten in the study site school. Eve observed with two different teachers: one, Mickie, was a special education teacher working with a Behaviorially and Emotionally Disturbed (BEH) class. The other, Donna, was the teacher in charge of the Chapter 1 remedial reading classroom. They each had less than ten years of teaching experience, several of which had been spent in schools other than the study site.

I came late to the project, beginning my work in the school midway through the school year in January, and conducted all of my observations in Sally's classroom, which I inherited from Dean, who went on to interview the faculty around the issue of professionalism. I have had prior teaching experience in several settings, including a public secondary school, a private art museum, and a university.

In order to more fully explore how we defined our roles in our respective observational settings, and to further determine where we located ourselves on that continuum of involvement and participation, I conducted multiple extended interviews over the year with each of my colleagues. Another source of data I found useful were the discussions that took place during our weekly team meetings, where we talked about both methodological and conceptual issues related to our work. I also made extensive use of my own personal classroom observations, analyzing my fieldnotes, a process that allowed me to look at the development of my own understandings. Finally, I asked Dean to interview me, using the protocol for the last round of researcher interviews I conducted.

I have just now begun the process of sharing the transcripts of the interviews. As we proceed with the arduous process of analyzing our fieldnotes, I hope the understandings I have gleaned from this study will continue to be useful in allowing us to own up to ourselves and the relationships we entered into in our work. I also trust that sharing these understandings will be helpful to the greater academic community as we attempt to come to common understandings of *caring*. My intention here is to put the "political moment" that Gitlin, Siegel, and Boru (1989) refer to in their discussion of "the politics of method" back into considerations of our work by encouraging a dialogue that will lead to a "shared mutual construction of understanding" (p. 238).

COMMANDMENTS AND COMMUNION

As we entered into the constant process of negotiating our locations and roles, a fundamental concern was the nature of the other parties involved in that negotiation process—our teachers and their students. Researchers—consciously or not—constantly consider competing images of responsibility as they variously define themselves as researchers or as adults, as caring or just, or as some collage of those images. This negotiation takes place in the process of communion with our participants, ourselves, and our images of ourselves as researchers and adults, and during this study it led to different limits or boundaries of responsibility and reciprocity for each of the researchers on the team. Wayne, whose experience closely related to that of the teacher he was observing, clearly and firmly located himself at one end of the spectrum of involvement as represented by the team members, while Dean was at the opposite end. In describing his activities in Martha's classroom, Wayne revealed that he moved from one image to another:

> It's changed somewhat over time. . . . I guess why I'm saying it's changed a bit is I have about stopped taking fieldnotes, I've just been acting more as the teaching assistant.

Dean, when asked to describe what kinds of things he did in the classroom, said:

> Observe. Period. I didn't help, or get involved in the activities or anything like that. . . . I never got involved in Sally's lessons; I felt she didn't want me to, and I didn't feel comfortable doing that. I didn't think that was one of my roles there as a researcher.

Whether owing to the more limited amount of time he spent in Sally's classroom, to the nature of his relationships in that classroom, to his inexperience with children at this grade level, or to his own personal research ethic, the self-image Dean shared here remained relatively stable. Located somewhere between the two extremes just described is John, who talked about how his location had shifted up and down the spectrum. John obviously adjusted his role according to what he perceived as his ability to participate appropriately at the time, and felt that his ability was limited by his lack of experience with children:

> I used to cruise the room helping out with the worksheets; I actually was *causing* trouble [rather] than solving any problems,

because I couldn't make the distinction between when the kids needed help and when they just wanted contact. And, that's a decision . . . that's a decision that the teachers have learned that I still don't know.

John's experiences with the children reinforced his perception of his inadequacies:

I got a lot of hugs, right. I was the lunchroom hit, that was the big, the big conflict among the children over who got to sit with me at lunch. Not because I could talk to them about anything. Because I wasn't very good at, you know, talking to the kids . . . it's something I anticipated, but it's not something I realized how hard it could be.

John's sense of inadequacy, earned or not, was picked up on by the children, as related in his telling of an event on the playground:

One crying girl on my left hand, one crying girl on my right hand, and I'm trying to get the kids in line, and we're walking back to the school and Mary behind me goes, "Dr. Wentworth, you can't handle this." To which I responded, "You're right, Mary." Now that's a clear one, right? On the one hand I think I overrespond to it, on the other hand I don't think I have a routine for it.

While their locations may have differed, two things that clearly operated to define the role each researcher constructed in the context of his or her setting was the nature of the relationship with the teacher and with the children in their classrooms, and the sense of responsibility those relationships carried with them. Eve observed in two different classrooms, (with two different teachers). Her relationship with each of these teachers was quite different, as was her location and role as researcher in their classrooms. With one teacher she described an instant rapport, a feeling of closeness and communion:

I would say what sticks out in my mind for Mickie's class is that I entered there, and Mickie and I immediately clicked, in terms of establishing this communication, this open communication. . . .

And the thing that struck me about her was just that she was so concerned about the students.

Eve described the outcome of her negotiation of location in Mickie's classroom as: "I don't really observe in a detached way; what happens is I observe as an aide." One constant in Eve's considerations was her responsibility to the children; as she said, a major factor in her participation was her duty to "make myself available to the students—definitely."

The location Eve described was very similar to that of Wayne, who also assisted with monitoring children's work, offered help with individual children, occasionally delivered instruction, and constantly made himself available "just to talk with the kids." Wayne illustrated the strong sense of responsibility he felt as a result of the relationships he had entered into:

> especially through observations, you know, doing fieldnotes, there's a need to want to be in relationships with kids and feeling responsive to the teacher, rather than just sitting back taking notes. . . . I'm learning about the dilemmas of caring, and when you care, you feel guilty when you don't feel like you're doing enough.

Eve also shared:

> If a student seemed particularly needful, I found myself trying to talk to them. Not in any way that had any long-lasting impact but as sort of a Band-Aid. . . . I felt like I had to; I could provide them some kind of temporary relief and I wanted to do that for them.

An interesting similarity between Wayne and Eve's contexts was that both Wayne and Eve felt very comfortable, perhaps even compelled, to engage as active participants (mostly as teacher assistants) in classrooms where their own teaching experience helped them to strongly identify with the teacher and where they felt able to make a positive contribution. Their ability to participate, in turn, allowed for the further development of relationships in those classrooms. Several considerations, however, beyond simply sharing a similar teaching history appeared to be operating here; one was their genuine admiration for the work they saw these teachers doing. Wayne, for example, had these perceptions of Martha and her teaching:

> Well, I'm just always amazed at Martha's teaching, and I just enjoy being in there because she's such a, a master at what . . . she really is able . . . my problem as a teacher is I would never . . . I never could figure, I never figured I set the right structure for the kids. I was always too nice, I couldn't get that "good-mean" sort of down. She, she's got that down; and the kids, you can see how well the kids respond to that.

Another of those considerations so well illustrated above was Wayne's explicit comparison of himself and his perception of his own teaching abilities with his perception of Martha. The pivotal point seemed to be the researcher's personal identification with the teacher's style. Inherent in both Eve's relationship with Mickie and Wayne's relationship with Martha was the clear understanding that they would "do it the same way," although perhaps not as well, as they perceived their teachers to be "doing it."

This identification and approval seemed to lead these researchers to define somewhat broader limits of responsibility, while the lack of such identification seemed to discourage participation. The stark contrast between Eve's experiences with Mickie and her experiences with Donna were a case in point. In Mickie's class she identified closely with the teaching style; as Eve said, she and Mickie were both "behavior mod" people, concerned with addressing the individual, special needs of their students. And they shared a philosophy about instruction that led to individualization and ultimately to greater researcher access:

> At times she [Mickie] wants me to do something with the students, or I'll see something going on with a student, and she's busy with another one, cause it's all very individualized; and so I'll just come in and help the student.

One the other hand, Eve clearly did not feel comfortable in Donna's class, did not identify with her style or philosophy, and therefore defined and located her limits accordingly:

In the other class [Donna's class] I sit in the back and strictly observe and have had very limited interaction with the students, because it's a very structured program with minimal individualization.

Really, being a second adult in that kind of environment, I've had to really make sure I don't change her [Donna's] focus, and I've had to ask her permission when I have helped students.

After one of those rare occasions when Eve asked Donna's permission to help the students with their work, she reported that Donna: "Approached me and said, 'You must think it's awful that I don't help them sound out the words.' " And so it would seem safe to assume that comparison and identification was a two-way street, that the teachers were very much aware of that process and that these negotiated relationships were essentially reciprocal.

TESTIFYING

When asked how they knew they had indeed "gotten close" to teachers and children, these researchers referenced a wide variety of experiences, as well as subtle embedded cues that were part of the social contracts they had established. These experiences and cues revealed or testified to their understanding that their access had been extended. John:

there was a point, somewhere this winter, in which Pam started talking to me over the classroom for the first time, and really did start talking to me more . . . the longer I'm there she lets more go. Like occasionally she will get what she calls "get ugly" with the kids while I'm there . . . she, that, I think for a long time she wouldn't do that when I was around and now she will; and I take that as an indication of trust.

And Eve:

It's very easy to give them [the children] my attention without feeling I'm overstepping my boundaries with Mickie . . . we've come to work as a team of teachers, and we would just naturally fill in for each other . . . and when she was sick one day, and I told her to go home, she was concerned because there wouldn't be a substitute teacher and I said, "I'll substitute, don't worry." And she *reluctantly* [laughs] conceded and left.

Finally, Wayne shared an experience that occurred nearly nine months after the completion of data collection—testifying to the continuity of his relationship with his teacher:

With Martha, well, she called me the other day to talk, because she's really considering not teaching anymore. And she wanted to talk to me about it. I took that as a compliment.

While all of these researchers were flattered by the indication of trust implicit in these interactions, only Eve and Wayne seemed fully secure in the equality of their relationships with their teachers. John described his understanding of the limits of his role with Pam:

She doesn't want me to do too much, because she wants me to stay her guest. Always stay in that client role, rather than, she doesn't want me to become a patron. And she certainly doesn't want me to become an equal. I can be her guest, I can be her respected guest, I can be her nice guest, right, all those, but I do not believe she wants my role to change from that of guest. It's kind of like, you know when you're a guest in someone's house, you make your bed?

John further shared his understanding of his role as guest:

I feel artificial when I'm talking to her. And part of it is I can't really take a role in the classroom. Part of it is that she is the most powerful teacher in the school, and I am her guest, and I always feel real conscious of my status as guest. And so, somewhat in the same way, you know, if you're at a formal dinner and you engage in polite conversation? I always feel that I'm bound by polite conversation rules.

The limitations of his relationship with Pam were also, at least in part, consciously accepted by John:

> I think we both would have liked to have been closer, but neither of us could really figure out how to do that. . . . Part of it on my end was, here's a woman in control of the school and, I felt that, for me to develop some affection or relationship with her might be interpreted as diminishing her, right? That was my, mine in doing that, I felt like I had to give her respect.

John also revealed his regret that those boundaries existed, comparing his relationship with Pam to that of Wayne's with Martha:

> They did get rather close over the course of the year, so I feel on that end there was something denied me. Not by Pam, but by the situation. . . . I certainly have no sense of being intimate with anyone there, right? I think that's different for Wayne, I think he was established an intimacy with Martha, and that's . . . and he is much better at that than I, that's not one of my strengths.

Dean, who did not participate in the life of the class while he was observing, compared his role to that of John and Wayne, saying: "They're doing so much more than just their work." I found this to be a telling statement because it reinforced Dean's earlier comment that he didn't perceive participation to be "one of [his] roles there as a researcher." Unlike John, Dean did not regret the limits of his involvement with Sally, perhaps because he felt those limits were natural and that they respected Sally's authority: "Probably everything that was done in there [in Sally's classroom] while I was observing was done on her terms."

Dean did, however, interpret the willingness of the teachers in the school to allow him to conduct interviews with them as evidence of having "gotten close," in a less intense and larger sense. When asked who he had gotten close to, and how did he know he was close, Dean shared the following comment about Serita, a teacher who felt very strongly that she had been misrepresented in the history of the school mentioned above:

The fact that these teachers let me interview them, the fact . . . the fact that Serita, after all the fallout from that history book that disturbed her, that she still allowed me to come and do an interview, and has told me that I'm welcome to come back and do others.

Dean also perceived an extension of trust in terms of the nature of what teachers were willing to disclose in those interviews. As he put it, he knew he'd gotten close because "they were willing to tell me some things that they knew were controversial, and they told me anyway."

At times getting close, like caring, can have its dark side. Just as caring too much or inappropriately in relationships can be controlling or instrumental, getting too close can also lead to unintended consequences. Researchers concerned with getting close may forget to revisit the commandment "do not intrude" and thus may violate the boundaries of their location in the field. Both Dean and John perceived that their presence was felt in some way, however slight, in their classrooms by their teachers. Dean stated:

I don't think I altered Sally's classroom much, I think Sally was generally minding her p's and q's more when I was there . . . although I don't think she ever saw me as an evaluator, I think that atmosphere was present when I was in the room . . . but not to the point that it altered the classroom. It was just a sense that there was some change in her personality.

And John said:

I'm sure Pam was more guarded when I was in her room than she is on the days when I was in her room than she is on the days when I wasn't there, right? In the interviews with the kids one of the things they would say they didn't like was the teacher screaming at you. Now, I only one time saw that.

While these subtle reminders of the capacity of getting close to change the setting were seen as natural and to be expected, what took researchers by surprise were the considerable effects of getting close in relationships in the classroom. Getting close to individuals and getting close to the community of the classroom was often inextricably tied to caring.

WITNESSING

I began this chapter with the metaphor of commandments, an overt (if light-hearted) religious metaphor and one that seemed particularly apt in view of the way, as researchers, we have often approached our fieldwork. For those of us with enough classroom experience to understand the complexity of the work teachers do, it was a truly awe-inspiring experience to witness the teachers in our study dealing with the demanding day-to-day world of their classrooms; for those with significant experience in similar classrooms, it was a time to reaffirm their faith. And, for the one team member with no prior direct experience with children in classrooms, it was a time to become more familiar with the rituals of an unfamiliar religion.

Witnessing then, has two meanings here: first, it means we saw evidence of caring and came to understand what caring meant in the context of what we were witnessing, in the sense of seeing. Second, we witnessed caring in much the same way that traditional Baptists engage in witnessing when they accept and begin to practice the tenets of their faith; as we became more comfortable with our faith, we began to practice it individually, consciously entering into caring interactions with the children. These interactions had a great deal to do with the way we have come to (re)define ourselves and to better understand the focus of this study. And, while I am not certain that we now have a clear understanding of all we know and have witnessed, we do have the beginning of shared meaning: in our attempt to define caring, we have said a great deal about ourselves, our responsibilities as adults to the children we have interacted with, and our ongoing responsibility to our own work.

It is, perhaps, telling that at least two "official" meanings of caring seem to be somewhat congruent with Gilligan's two ethics: Caring as charge, protection, or custody, and caring as liking or regard. Caring, for teachers and for researchers, it seems can be all or any combination of these. When I first interviewed my fellow researchers, asking what caring meant to them, they responded as follows. Eve:

> Caring means that you can communicate to another person that you're truly concerned about them. And that whatever role you're in, whatever your relationship is with them, that you're going to try your best to be sensitive to their needs.

Wayne:

> I think it has something to do with concern. But, you have to act on that concern. So I think it's, I guess in terms of a, of a researcher in the classroom, what caring means is that kids come—and Martha comes—before the research does.

John:

> Oh God! Well, it has a couple of meanings to me. One is that it's something about affect, but, what I think I've learned is affect never exists separate[ly]. Particularly in the teach[er]–student relationship, it's always affect in the context of doing something; let's say either more instrumental or substantive . . . and I think I didn't know that before this . . . this study.

And from Dean, the response was a revealing: "I know it when I see it." When I followed up on this response, asking him what it was that he had seen, he replied:

> Well, I can tell you what teachers have told me, but that's not the same thing as how do I feel about caring. Caring interactions that I've seen are the pats on the back, and the teacher . . . the fact that Sally told me that story, about that boy [who was having a difficult time in class due to personal problems at home], I think is caring for him, and caring about the whole process of education, because she wanted to share that story. And one thing about Sally, because she's a fairly, I talked about her control and the fact that she is an authority in that classroom, but yet she is, she is very soft-spoken with the students . . . and there's a certain

amount of caring that goes into that, because she's very calm with those students, she doesn't embarrass the students, doesn't violate their sense of integrity.

Dean added:

Of course in the interviews I don't see caring interactions, but I think it's interesting that all these teachers talk about their relationships. They seldom talk about instructional methods or subject matter; it's almost always about relationships. [And when describing caring to him] they described caring acts, acts of caring. Which I think is subtly different than caring itself.

Nearly one year later, when asked what caring meant to him, Dean himself talked about relationships:

well, right at this particular minute, I think it means attempting to understand, or allow somebody to understand why it is that they interpret . . . the world in a certain way. And holding their interpretation as important, not that you have to accept it as true, or as the one interpretation, but that you place some importance on the fact that person has a perception or an interpretation, that has an effect on your relationship with them. And on their relationships with other people.

Of all the researchers Dean was the least invested in the notion that caring is, or should be, an integral part of the life of classrooms, a notion the other researchers seemed willing to own as a taken-for-granted assumption. He was, therefore, the most difficult to convince, or perhaps convert. In fact, during his interviews with the teachers when caring was mentioned by the participants, he would apologize for asking them to elaborate, saying: ''I have to ask you this for John and Wayne, you also said a good teacher is one who cares about kids. Can you tell me what that means?'' When all the teachers he spoke with testified to the importance of caring to the work they do with children, to their efforts towards professionalism, and to their sense of moral responsibility, and when caring unmistakably emerged from his data, only then did Dean begin to accept and to testify to the importance of caring in the context of classrooms. His distinctly humorous introduction of the issue of caring is several recent presentations of his work on the professionalization of teaching attests to his conversion: Dean now stands up and proudly confesses, "I am Dean Deland, and I am a Caring Theorist!"

Each researcher working on the Caring Study has experienced, directly or vicariously, moments when knowing and action merged into acts of caring. Eve described her understanding of caring by relating some of those moments:

> When I see students help one another with their work; when they don't laugh when a student has made an obvious, blatant mistake, and the kids don't laugh. And, the same thing on the teacher's part as well, when the teacher allows the child to recuperate and save face.

Eve also touched on the reciprocal nature of these acts of caring:

> There also, there seems, it's so difficult to describe and put my finger on it, but there seems to be this agreement in classrooms that the teacher is there to help the students grow, and the students are there to allow the teacher to find fulfillment in knowing that he or she is making a difference.

For Eve "finding fulfillment" was also a personal issue, and she now knows that fulfillment for her comes from her relationships with her participants:

> I must find ways that I—this sounds selfish, but it's true—ways that I can enjoy the setting; that I can relate and connect with the people . . . and if I can't I don't know how, I don't think I'd be able to do it.

In addition to his perception that caring is "something about affect" and that "it's always affect in the context of doing something," John also said caring is: "a way for me to talk about what goes on between teachers and students with one, with one term." When I asked him to describe interactions he had participated in that he would characterize as caring, he talked about his relationship with one little boy, a student that he perceived as needy. The caring was expressed in actions such as those he describes here:

> Well, there was clearly one boy in the classroom that he and I have some relationship . . . he's not the best student, and he can act out plenty and all that kind of stuff . . . he always wants to sit with me at lunch, and he makes a lot of eye-contact with me during the course of the day. And if he's not feeling well, has an earache or something, will tell me . . . so that's an ongoing relationship. I will wink at him when he's upset and stuff like that so he and I have, like, whatever that is, I think that's caring. He knows that I pay attention to him, and he pays attention to me, and we seem to like each other.

Wayne, in response to a request to describe caring interactions he has had, referred to a particular student, Alex:

> I think he's failed; I know he's failed at least once, and he may have been held back two grades, and at the beginning of this year he could barely read . . . [describing the interaction]I think the one with Alex maybe, when we worked on that book. Only because it was something, it was something he wanted to do. And, I guess, it—I—the only reason I'm saying it's caring is because I took the time to really do that with him, I was there anyway; I'm not sure that it was caring in that I went out of my way to do . . . but I took time away from what, from my taking fieldnotes . . . but just helping him to be able to work through this book and be able to write this story for some reason meant a lot, a lot to him; it just—the fact that I was able to do that, I guess, was just because I cared about him.

Clear perception of need is an important factor in the initiation of acts of caring, both for teachers and researchers. As visitors to the classrooms, these researchers in particular attended to the needy children, the Alexes who can't read or have been held back, those who "aren't the best students," those who "act out," those children with easily identified emotional and academic needs. I found it significant that both Dean and I, having observed in the same classroom, singled out the same boy to attend to. While I am sure part of that was owing to the physical proximity of Mark's desk to the table where we sat to take our notes, I am equally aware that it was also due in large part to our independent perceptions of this child's unmistakable need. Mark was in the "slow" reading group and had obvious difficulty reading aloud; he was therefore allowed quite a bit of latitude by Sally, and both of these conditions tended to single him out. Perhaps—most importantly—Mark initiated his own contact with us, establishing eye-contact, visiting us at our table and entering into brief conversations concerning our roles in the classroom. Dean describes:

> There was a—the first time I observed—there was a kid named Mark who was in Sally's room, and he was in the back corner of the room, and he seemed to always be involved in some kind of mischief . . . and Sally said nothing to him . . . and he was asked to read; and I remember he had a hard time . . . and Sally helped him along. And then the second time I went in to observe, this same kid came over to me and asked me what I was doing.

After several visits—and notes that match Dean's description of his experiences with Mark—I had the following experience when Mark came to the back of the room and sat beside me to work on an art project:

> I commented on what a good job he'd done with the face he'd drawn, and he smiled. He got a pair of scissors out . . . and began scratching lines into the india ink he had painted over the crayon design. . . . He worked for a little while and then stopped and looked at what he'd done, shaking his head and rubbing his finger over some of the lines he'd made. He turned and looked up at the . . . example the art teacher had left . . . and then back at his picture. I asked him if he was having some trouble getting his lines straight and he said, "Yes." I picked up a ruler and held it on his drawing while he drew with the scissors, and then we talked about how he could paint back over the section he'd been having trouble with. I . . . . went out into the hallway to see if any of the girls had finished with a paintbrush so that Mark could use it; Tonya said she was almost done, and I asked her to please save it for Mark.

My decision to become closely involved, to participate in what I would consider to be a caring act, was based on several considerations, the first of which was my perception of Mark's need, the second, my knowledge that I could, in fact, readily do something to help him, and the third, my understanding that by coming to sit by me he was extending the limits of my responsibility or obligation to him as a child in relation to me as an adult. He was "affording me access," in much the same way that the other researchers reported children in their classrooms extended invitations to "get close," to care. And, when I received his invitation, I felt obliged to adjust my location and respond—witnessing, in the Baptist sense, what I understood about caring and its responsibilities.

GRACE

Give back was a phrase that was often used by members of the Caring Study team when discussing issues of reciprocity. Giving back to the field and our participants seemed to have two levels of meaning; one was a bread-and-butter thank-you, as evidenced by John, who said at the end of data collection:

> My biggest query now is, What can I do that Pam will appreciate? Right? That I can somehow, "give" her is the wrong word, but I think it conveys the sentiment, right? You know, that I can give her for being so good to me. . . . I gave her a copy of Among Schoolchildren . . . which I signed, "from your oldest student," right?

Beyond simple appreciation is giving back in terms of sharing knowledge, informing action, merging meaning and application if at all possible. While bread-and-butter giving back would be merely gracious, sharing knowledge is somehow mutually gratifying. Dean expressed his concern with this sort of giving back:

> I'm concerned that they find the interview process useful, that they get something out of the interview and that they're not just talking to me, that their talking about this is useful to them.

While we were in the field, a kind of protection became a mechanism for giving back. For example, John shared that his concern with the ramifications of his very public alliance with the principal in the school:

> made me have to do some things that I normally wouldn't have done. Normally, I would never have said anything about what was going on in the classroom or anything [to the principal], but it made me praise Pam in his presence. I felt that I had to do that.

In my own interview I shared the same concern with giving protection:

> I noticed right away, and I don't know if this had to so with having been a teacher or if it just had to do with the nature of the fact that I felt like the teacher and the kids were vulnerable in some fashion; and I think it was a combination of both, but I was very protective of what went on in that classroom. And I would not mention [to the principal] anything unless I could make a very positive comment. But if I could I would give him something positive.

Regardless of our attempts at bread-and-butter thank-yous and protection, I do not believe any of us felt that we had done enough; we were not, in fact, sufficiently gratified by our small attempts to inform our participants or by our efforts to allow their participation to be meaningful, both to them and to the research.

KNOW THYSELF

In order to "make the familiar strange" (Erickson, 1973), the familiar being the classroom context and culture I was to observe, I had to prepare for my journey by "packing my bags," by acknowledging my taken-for-granteds and tacit assumptions. Once, when preparing for a long trip, a friend told me that, in order to make sure my baggage would be manageable, "pack everything you think you will need—and then leave three-fourths of that behind.'' When I journeyed into Sally's class-room, I tried to follow my friend's advice: I tried to bring with me only that baggage that might be useful—my own teaching experience, my sense of self as a teacher, and a little experience as a researcher. My sense of self as a researcher was not nearly so well defined nor clearly articulated as my "teacher understand-ings,'' but I had some beginnings that I thought I might use.

What I tried to leave behind was my near-overwhelming capacity for immediate involvement: I have a long history as a compulsive volunteer! Early on, when planning my approach to the classroom, to the teacher, and to the community of students in that classroom, I decided I should stay out of the setting until I knew exactly where I was. Then, with that location firmly grounded in my observations, I would cross the narrow and much-contested border into direct classroom involvement and attempt to get close—while not intruding.

As related earlier, I inherited my observation site in Sally's classroom from Dean. When I entered her classroom I knew what relationships already existed between the researcher and the participants in that context; and, while I certainly had to enter into my own negotiations and then to locate myself accordingly, I already was carrying with me an image of what was acceptable there. Originally I made a considered decision not to make substantial changes, a decision based on several factors, fore-most among them that I was a novice field researcher, and that strict observation is much more clear-cut than participation. The second factor had to do with what I saw as my responsibility to continue to provide data consistent with Dean's for the good of the team. The final, and most important, factor to be considered had to do with Sally's and the children's perception of my role and the amount of access and participation that they were comfortable with. And so, in the beginning I sat at my table at the back of the room and stayed out of the life of the classroom:

> I try to be as unobtrusive as possible, particularly until I establish some sort of relationship with Sally, but it's really hard not to want to get involved. Several times I found myself experiencing a strong urge to get up and walk around the room and look at what they're [the children] reading or working on, or just ask a

question, but right now I don't want to do anything but just observe.

As time went on I changed my location on the spectrum of involvement, in large part owing to the relationship that developed between Sally and me, and to the invitations extended by some of the children, such as Mark, and also because of my identification with at least some elements of Sally's teaching style:

> While I know I'm never as "in control" as Sally, I do think we share some characteristics—like lots of immediate positive reinforcement, and constant monitoring, walking up and down the aisles, and always being available to the kids. Also, I am impressed that she is so open to the kids' doing artwork whenever they have a minute.

It was, in fact, a shared interest in art that really led to Sally's inviting me fully into the life of the class:

> Sally asked me to come and observe an extra day this week so that I could see the art teacher do a lesson with the kids. She also wanted to know if I would like to do something with them before the end of the year, and we're going to talk about it while I'm there next time.

When I made the decision to accept that invitation, I reconsidered many of those limiting and locating factors presented above, and I revisited my original commandments. That process finally led to my realization that it was time to give something back, not only to Sally, but to the children as well. During my last visit to the classroom I shared my research with them, in a presentation that celebrated the life of their class—my own bread-and-butter thank you. But, somehow, I knew that wasn't enough; that had been gracious, but it wasn't gratifying.

In her essay "How Fieldwork Changed Me," Rosalie Wax shares this revelation:

A colleague has suggested that I reflect on the extent to which I was changed as a person by doing fieldwork. I reflected, and the result astonished me. For what I realized was that I had not been greatly changed by the things I suffered, enjoyed or endure; nor was I greatly changed by the things I did (though these strengthened my confidence in myself). What changed me irrevocably and beyond repair were the things I learned. (1971, p. 363)

Research is a process, and process implies change; in order to understand how I have changed as a result of my work, I took the advice offered above and reflected on what I had learned. My results reassure me: The next time I prepare to journey into the field, I hope to be better prepared to understand what I will find there. My baggage has been altered beyond repair and on my next journey I will take what I have learned as it has now become a part of who I am.

So, in what ways have I changed? What have I learned? First, I learned how important it is to define yourself, to acknowledge your own subjectivity; that, beyond knowing where you are on your journey into the field, you must know *who* you are each step of the way. Researchers must make a concerted effort to know themselves and know how and why they are represented in the research: examining the nature of their communion with participants, and reflecting on the manner in which they testify to their relationships and witness what they have learned. This process of self-definition and owning up becomes imperative as researchers begin to cross that fine line, to indeed follow the commandment to get close.

In addition to learning that I felt very strongly that knowing where and who you are in the research is important, I also learned that I would like to feel as if my work had made a difference, that I had something useful to say, particularly to those people who so gladly informed me. I learned that I think an unfortunate, self-imposed limitation of some ethnographic research is the separation of "understanding and application," even as I recognized that "questions about whether to intervene in a culture and what kinds of social relations to enter into with members of the culture are essential for all ethnographers" (Gitlin et al., 1989, pp. 242-239). Saying grace should be more than a gentle thank you; it should be heartfelt and gratifying.

Another lesson learned has to do with the political nature of all research and the overwhelming need to consider the ethical implications of conducting research, whatever the setting, whoever the participants, regardless of the focus. But perhaps the most valuable lesson I learned is one that compels me to add one final commandment to our stone tablet; I learned that considerations of locations, role, responsibility and participation should be undertaken with not only justice, but with care; and so the last commandment must read, "Consider with care."

REFERENCES

Eisner, E. W., & Peshkin, A. (1990). *Qualitative inquiry in education: The continuing debate.* New York: Teachers College Press.

Erickson, F. (1973). What makes school ethnography ethnographic? *Council on Anthropology and Education Newsletter, 2,* 10–19.

Gilligan, C. (1982). *In a different voice.* Cambridge, MA: Harvard University Press.

Gitlin, A., Siegel, M., & Boru, K. (1989) The politics of method: From leftist ethnography to educative research. *Qualitative Studies In Education, 2*(3), 237–253.

Patton, M. Q. (1990). *Qualitative evaluation and research methods.* Newbury Park, CA: Sage.

Wax, R. (1971). *Doing fieldwork.* Chicago: University of Chicago Press.

Chapter 8

Transformational Caring: Women's Voices Within Academe

Deborah J. Eaker

INTRODUCTION

Carol Gilligan (1982) has argued that our society and educational institutions are lacking an "ethic of caring." This chapter will examine this critique. First I must say that I disagree with Gilligan: I maintain that it is *not* the case that an ethic of caring is missing, but rather than it has heretofore been characterized by a simplistic social discourse. Furthermore, although Nel Noddings (1984) has explored the philosophical complexity of this ethic in an educational context, I believe that there remains an "audible silence" (Bowers, 1984) in the daily manifestations of social caring due to a lack of grounded studies. I contend that a progressively complex, dynamic, and informed view of caring within education must consider the material, structural, and ideological relations of the daily lives of students and educators. Such a consideration demands that potentially dissonant voices must be allowed and heard. This chapter indicates that the simplistic social discourse about caring intentionally or unintentionally masks power relationships. Furthermore, this chapter explores the power relationships for tenured women in academe and gives voice to a concept of caring as transformational, a previously unexplored idea within the context of higher education.

This work represents a piece of a larger study that investigated the schooling and career experiences of black and white tenured women who have been termed *successful* in the normative sense of the academy (Eaker, 1990). The larger study informed our understandings of success by illuminating the ways currently held assumptions, hypotheses, and theories of women in academe are incomplete explanations. For the overall study, qualitative in-depth interviews, termed *educational life history*, were conducted with 12 tenured women (six Caucasians and six African-Americans all 39 to 53 years old and most in their mid to late 40s) from one public Category I university. The disciplines represented by these women were primarily the social sciences and humanities, since women, as a group, are more widely represented, and have participated for longer periods of time, in these disciplines. These 12 women were questioned about specific schooling experiences, major influences on these experiences of schooling, and their subsequent academic careers. They spoke about their careers in terms of its rewards and sacrifices.

All interviews took place in the faculty offices of the individual respondents. The average length of the interviews was 90 minutes. The interviews were conducted between June 1989 and February 1990. All interviews were transcribed verbatim and analyzed by the researcher for recurring themes and categories. These accounts were then used as the basis for comparison with other accounts and theories purported to explain the experiences and data on academic women.

The data in this chapter were gathered from three questions summarized here: How do you most like to work? Do you feel successful as an academic (and if yes, how and why)? From what do you get your motivation—the spark—the desire to do what you do? The answers to these questions revealed professional orientations that challenged previous interpretations, particularly in regard to the pedagogical relationships of women with their students and their sense of personal and collective agency. It is these particular aspects of these women's lives that lead to this discussion of, and challenge to, the traditional notion of caring in the realms of higher education. In the following sections, I will explore the notions of caring and agency through use of specific portions of the narratives of the 12 women interviewed. Pseudonyms will be used in the recounting of these narratives; distinctions of race will be noted only where deemed important to the reader's understandings.

ORIENTATION TO STUDENTS: A COMMITMENT TO MENTOR AND TO EMPOWER

In Jesse Bernard's landmark study (1964), academic women were portrayed as being in nontraditional roles for women yet as still performing traditional female functions in their nurturing and support of students. Perhaps this was indeed the functions female academics felt themselves to be performing in the 1960s. Conversely, this may also be an instance of fitting the evidence to a stereotype, as Jane Roland Martin (1985) suggests is often the case. In any event, despite their obvious voiced commitment to students, none of these women see their primary function with their students as being that of nurturance and support. Rather, what they are committed to providing for students is mentoring and personal empowerment.

A Commitment to Mentoring

All of these women mentioned students as being extremely important in their professional lives and a source of professional reward. However, several of them specifically speak of a commitment to mentoring as a part of their orientation to students. Evelyn Fox Keller (1977) characterized herself, along with other academic women she has known, as women who, because they have male aspirations to succeed in academics, have had little sense of sisterhood. Perhaps, since Keller is a woman in the "hard sciences," her experience of other female academics was different or perhaps there has been a shift in the past decade; in either case, the women interviewed here have a strong orientation to students, particularly to female students. One gets a sense of their "being a symbol or model for possibilities or potential ways of being in the world as a woman" (Weiler, 1988, pp. 116).

Dr. Sarah Cook, whose experience in graduate school and

academe has been one of having no professional mentors, believes herself and others to be role models for women students. She characterizes the present situation for women graduate students as very different from her own situation. She sees herself as making the way of an academic career less difficult for her women graduate students. She describes it in this manner.

> I think that now we as women professors with our women graduate students—they are very much aware that what they might do might embarrass us, that we're proud of them that they're out there. We're helping them, we're paving the way for them, they're conceived as an extension of us.

Dr. Patricia Miller is even more explicit about her mentoring role. She purposefully picks out students to mentor; she talks of the commitment she has made to these mentoring relationships.

> [I mentor] one female graduate student a year. I've done that for about 3 years now—consciously—I think I was doing that before. . . . [I think it's important that there be] just some female faculty who has achieved—not only career-wise—but has achieved the respect of her colleagues [and] is investing that kind of time.

She goes on to explain her commitment to women and the significance of this mentoring to the lives of women graduate students. In describing her choice of the yearly female graduate student, she says,

> it's typically a woman who does not know how good she is because she hasn't been told. A woman who's already gotten her life together has gotten it somewhere along the line. . . . I just flat won't back out on a woman. It's that simple. It's just the bottom line.

For Dr. Susan Gantt, the commitment to students is evident. However, her words also recall the dilemma of women academics who are so often called upon in this regard. She explains that mentoring is

something I want to be a part of my job . . . partly because I feel
like people did this for me and it's my turn to give back. I had real
good role models. So, I've got good ones I can be like. So, I think
for some I can do that well. My biggest problem is that I'm going
to have to limit whom I can do that for.

For these women, mentoring students is a high priority
despite the time investment and conflict this commitment sometimes entails. For others, a commitment to the personal empowerment of students is their challenge.

A Commitment to Personal Empowerment

The commitment to personal empowerment for their students is
not unrelated to that of mentoring and, in fact, those who speak
of mentoring as a commitment see personal empowerment as
one of the logical outcomes of their mentoring relationships.
Patricia Miller is one who believes this is part of her mentoring
process. She says of herself that "I strongly believe in empowerment. . . . My goal is to make [my mentee] stronger in herself.
To teach her some things about where she can have relationships
with power."

Those who talk of empowerment outside of mentoring relationships speak of the professorial role as being more one of
enabling individual action by students. Dr. Anne Daniels, an
African-American, in speaking of her commitment to empower
individuals, laughingly says "I don't know anything about
being nurturing. You've got to get people through." She goes on
to explain what she calls her "business."

My business is about empowering people and individuals to make
decisions for themselves. . . . The bottom line is that it will
always be you. . . . I don't care what race, color, sex or whatever—these are going to be barriers, but you will have to do it for
yourself eventually. It's about *affecting individuals to take care of
themselves.* . . . I have those ideals [about the system changing],
and I am still idealistic, but it comes to the point of the individual
being responsible for himself or herself.

Finally, Dr. Margaret Jacobs speaks of the powerlessness she sees in some students. She almost grimaces as she talks.

It bugs me about young people I meet in universities that they are so easily made to feel powerless. That they are so quickly ready to give up the things that are right to hand that they could be doing. It's just not right. They shouldn't be made to feel powerless. I don't know what has led them to feel that they have so little that they can do, that they are somehow so isolated from the world.

This expression of her discontent that students are "made to feel powerless" hints at her belief in the empowering potential of pedagogy, a commitment expressed by many of these women.

ORIENTATION TO PEDAGOGY: THE POTENTIAL FOR PERSONAL AND SOCIAL TRANSFORMATION

Angela Simeone (1987) reports that at present, as in the past, academic women prefer teaching over other aspects of their jobs. This propensity toward teaching has historically been considered to be reflective of the presumed nurturing qualities of women. Additionally, academic women have been perceived as unwise in their preference for teaching. Particularly in research institutions this choice is seen as naive, since teaching is not rewarded, in these institutions, to the same degree as research and publication. As seen in the previous section, the women in this study have developed relationships with students out of a commitment to mentoring and empowerment. The same thread of commitment comes through in their talk about pedagogy. Their stories serve to place in doubt the presumption of the choice of teaching as nurturing: Additionally, they call into question the presumed relative value of teaching as a commitment. For these women, pedagogy holds the potential for both personal and social transformation.

The Potential for Personal Transformation

Aisenberg and Harrington (1988) relate that learning for many women is a transformational experience. Thus, they argue, "the lure of teaching for many women is the desire to reinvoke the transformational experience. . . . Women invoking change in others" (p. 39). They go on to claim that the transformative potential in pedagogy is in "the power of ideas and intellectual training" (p. 79). Dr. Sarah Cook hopes that she makes an intellectual difference for students to the extent that "they will come up with some whole new way to do [this] and that they will have to train themselves. [I hope] that they will reject what we've taught them."

Weiler (1988) argues that more than personal self-consciousness and critique is needed for true societal change to occur. However, she does admit that such self-critique is a necessary first step. The academic women here express this same notion of influencing the way students think about themselves and the world. They argue that pedagogy is an effective step by which to influence individuals: They believe that their teaching makes a difference in individual lives.

Dr. Anne Daniels, in reflecting on her professional contributions, states, "I have made my contribution even if it's been encouraging one individual to think about themselves a little bit differently." Dr. Miller believes that in her teaching "most of the time I'm making a difference for at least some people . . . and that's quite important to me. I can't think of another place where I could do that as much."

Although a distinction is made here, the realm of the personal is not divorced from that of the social and political contexts in which students live and study. Thus, these women also talk about the potential of pedagogy for social transformation.

The Potential for Social Transformation

Aisenberg and Harrington (1988) claim that very few women enter their professional lives with a view of themselves as agents of historical change or with a change agenda for professional practice. Rather, they argue, academic women follow their personal agendas. Certainly, the stories of these women are replete with their personal agendas but it is apparent in their conversations about pedagogy that they make a direct link between pedagogy and social transformation. Indeed, many strongly express this potential as the *primary* reason they value and give priority to the teaching aspects of their jobs. The priority and significance of teaching for Dr. Miller is summed up in her words that "a lot of my energies have been put into that route to affect a lot of people."

Dr. Zora Steele, an African-American, emphasizes the interrelationship of the personal with any sort of social transformation in her statements about teaching. She describes her teaching this way.

> I don't necessarily have an agenda, but I only teach the things that I know, and hopefully my knowledge is always expanding. But, basically, when we teach the things we know, we're teaching who we are. I don't think that in any of the classes I get away from doing that part of the job of teaching. So, some of the concerns, no matter what the course is, will have to deal with women, will have to deal with African-Americans, will have to deal with racism and sexism in society, will have to deal with elitism and classism and so on.

Dr. Margaret Jacobs expresses her belief in the importance of pedagogy for personal and social transformation. She speaks of the challenge it presents to her as a professor.

> I see pedagogy as a *very, very* important area for political action. A lot of kids come through this university and rising to the challenge of reaching them with something new, something that they haven't thought of before, something that might destabilize some of their common sense, is about as much as I ask of myself. But, I think it's good; I think it's important.

It is clear that, for Dr. Margaret Jacobs, and others, the transformative potential of pedagogy is seen as the main mechanism by which to enable any sort of effective social change. Dr. Jacobs continues:

> Where else is hegemony going to be influenced. I no longer believe in the efficiency of conventional political action. Our social order arises from an hegemony of values and of very deeply ingrained processes. . . . These practices have to be addressed

and I think the only way we're going to do that is by spending time making people question what they're doing in their ordinary lives.

Finally, for Dr. Patricia Miller, commitment to the potential of pedagogy for social transformation brings the juxtaposition of the personal and the political sharply into focus. It is in her pedagogy that she heals her own experiences of personal oppression. She speaks in a very deliberate, assured tone.

I really believe that [teaching] is one of the ways—probably the primary way—I make a difference in the world. . . . Scholarship, yes, but the teaching has such a direct impact. . . . I know I've made the difference in people's vision of that, awareness of [sexism]. . . . One of the ways I deal with the pain is with my commitments that the next generation of women won't have to experience this.

Dr. Miller's statement integrates the personal and social motivations behind the commitments seen in the professional lives of these women to their students and their pedagogy. These commitments serve to call into question the usual interpretations of academic women's relationships with their students and their dedication to pedagogy. Their sense of caring at this point in their lives of one of transformation engendered by an expanded and powerful sense of personal and collective agency.

TRANSFORMATIONAL CARING AND THE IMPLICATIONS FOR SCHOOLING AND SOCIETY

As stated throughout this chapter, women within academe are often criticized for the priority they give to students and teaching. In terms of the time and attention they invest in their students, previous interpretations within the literature have seen this as consistent with the "natural caring" evidenced in women. While these women certainly care *about* their students, they in no way indicate that they *take care of* their students. Their relationships with students are largely built upon their commitment to mentoring and student empowerment rather than for the purposes of nurturance and support as some studies have suggested (cf. Bernard, 1964). In fact, perhaps studies, such as those by Gilligan (1982) and Belenky, Clinchy, Goldberger, and Tarule (1986), fail to account for the effects of advanced education upon women. It could be speculated that what is often seen as natural caring among women is, in fact, a result of the class situation of the majority of women, which presupposes the care and nurturance of children and households. The influence of higher education for these women may, in fact, mitigate that class ideology at least in the way it is manifest with students.

Academic women are also often considered foolish and impractical in their preference for teaching rather than research. In this group of highly successful women, research is obviously a key commitment in their professional lives. Nonetheless, on balance, teaching is presumably their highest priority, as evidenced by the way in which they discuss teaching and the time they commit to teaching. However, once again, contrary to superficial interpretations, these women see pedagogy as enabling both personal and social transformation. Their professional commitment to the transformative potential of pedagogy contradicts the assumption that women in academe do not imagine themselves as "agents of significant historical change" (Aisenberg & Harrington, 1988, p. 19). Weiler (1988) indicates that "the question for women is how the human ability to create meaning and resist an imposed ideology can be turned into praxis and social transformation" (p. 50). For these academics, pedagogy is the empowering personal and social praxis that attempts to answer that question and provide possibilities for transformation.

In these narratives, which reveal so poignantly the professional commitments to students and pedagogy, there is a sense of these women seeing their prior personal and professional struggles in need of an individual solution with the total awareness that they represent women and/or people of color. Their solutions and commitments are thus made in light of this collective and group identity. Such a commitment, in fact, would be consistent with interpretations of women as acting out of a sense of caring about and in relationship to the world (cf. Chodorow, 1978) rather than merely out of a sense of personal relationship for the purpose of nurturance.

The implications for higher education given women with the commitments evident in the lives of these 12 are vast. As Weiler (1988) argues, merely "the presence of women or minorities in positions of power change the consciousness of everyone in a school, whether the presence of these people in these positions is *welcomed, accepted,* or *resisted* (p. 111; emphasis added). These women in higher education take their positions of power very seriously and do evidence a clear use of that power, albeit in the nontraditional, deceptively neutral use of their pedagogical skill and the freedom they exercise within their classrooms. The potential outcome for schooling and higher education of such an orientation to pedagogy as transformational is that of a change within the practice of gender in academe and the possibility for that change to be affected at a larger societal level. Within this expanded concept and practice of gender comes the opportunity for our discourse regarding caring to be seen in light of its full complexity, potential and value for a society of women and men who can acknowledge its possibility.

The lives of these 12 women are examples of a committed moral and ethical stance about human beings, education, and this society. The actions and language they use to frame their lives creates a *different possibility.* Dr. Katherine Owens, an African-American, is symbolic of the possibility seen in the lives of all twelve of these women as she talks of her own children: She retains her sense of anger and indignation at the inequalities she sees and experiences, but explains that "it's necessary to shelve . . . this from time to time and not to overpower their lives with it. . . . You can't raise kids on anger." Whether, like Dr. Owens, they speak of children of their own or the young adult children of other people, on balance, in their commitments to their profession these women manage to span the gap from critique to transformation. As such, they provide a grounded possibility for transformational caring.

REFERENCES

Aisenberg, N., & Harrington, M. (1988). *Women of academe: Outsiders in the sacred grove.* Amherst, MA: University of Massachusetts Press.
Belenky, M.F., Clinchy, B.M., Goldberger, N.R., & Tarule, J.M. (1986).

Women's ways of knowing: The development of self, voice, and mind. New York: Basic Books.

Bernard, J. (1964). *Academic women.* University Park, PA: Pennsylvania State University Press.

Bowers, C.A. (1984). *The promise of theory.* New York: Teachers College Press.

Chodorow, N. (1978). *The reproduction of mothering: Psychoanalysis and the sociology of gender.* Berkeley, CA: University of California Press.

Eaker, D.J. (1990). *'Becoming a different kind of person, making a different kind of world': Race, class and gender in the schooling and career experiences of twelve academic women.* Unpublished doctoral dissertation, University of North Carolina at Chapel Hill.

Gilligan, C. (1982). *In a different voice: Psychological theory and women's development.* Cambridge, MA: Harvard University Press.

Keller, E.F. (1977). The anomaly of a woman in physics. In S. Ruddick & P. Daniels (Eds.), *Working it out* (pp. 77-91). New York: Pantheon Books.

Martin, J.R. (1985). Becoming educated: A journey of alienation or integration? *Journal of Education, 167* (3), 71-83.

Noddings, N. (1984). *Caring: A feminine approach to ethics and moral education.* Berkeley, CA: University of California Press.

Simeone, A. (1987). *Academic women: Working towards equality.* South Hadley, MA: Bergin and Garvey.

Weiler, K. (1988). *Women teaching for change: Gender, class and power.* South Hadley, MA: Bergin and Garvey.

Conclusions

The Tapestry Completed (But Not Finished)

Deborah J. Eaker
A. Renee Prillaman

Throughout the chapters of this book, the authors have presented their own experiences of caring in educational contexts. These experiences illustrate and form the various strands of what we have termed the *tapestry of caring* in education. In this chapter, we will examine those strands, weave together common strands, and review the complete tapestry as we have come to understand it. We will do this through broadening our discussion of the technical and the expressive and looking at three aspects of weaving to which these notions can be applied. Finally, we will consider the implications of what this book has presented in terms of current educational theory and practice.

THE LANGUAGE OF THE TECHNICAL, THE LANGUAGE OF THE EXPRESSIVE: A REDEFINITION

In the introduction, we reviewed the literature of the past 20 years on effective teaching: This is what we termed the *language of the technical*. We proposed that this language continues to inform us about what certain appropriate practices might be in order for one to be considered technically effective as a teacher.

Danin's chapter, "Contradictions and Conflicts in Caring," delineates that aspect of educating we are referring to as the

191

technical. The language she uses refers to "goals, strategies, objectives, replicable models and evaluation." Some of the educators in her study were concerned with these aspects of teaching because they were objective and quantifiable. In Chapter 4, McLaughlin also describes the technical aspects of teaching, which he refers to as curricular caring. The aspects of the technical he describes are much like those of Goodman (1988) and Prillaman (1988), which include discipline, group control, planning, activities, and materials. McLaughlin is careful to point out that these aspects of teaching are not oppositional to caring. Rather, the mastery of these aspects of teaching is generally important to the caring teacher. However, the educators in both Danin's and McLaughlin's work would not consider mastery of the technical to be sufficient to create good teaching.

In addition to the language of the technical, we have examined the theoretical discourse on caring, a part of what we have termed the *language of the expressive.* Our expanded notions of caring and expressiveness entail the qualities of work and communication that are literally expressive of the deepest sense of self. In the case of it being self-expressive, we assert that the concept of self entails a cognition of "the other." At the same time, the language of expressiveness would not necessarily preclude what we might define culturally as individuality. Additionally, while not necessitating reason, the language of the expressive does not preclude reason as its base, although perhaps expanding the form or definition of reason.

In the example of McLaughlin's work previously mentioned, he discusses the value of a combination of technical and expressive aspects of education while he also points out the contrasting nature of the two. The student teachers in his study varied in their interpretations of caring for their students, but they did share in common a strong regard and appreciation of caring for their students. Danin also contrasts these aspects of teaching. Some of the teachers in her study were greatly concerned with the relational aspect of teaching and feared that requirements of the new project they had taken on would interfere with what they considered to be the more important part of their work. Danin uses Noddings's term *authentic caring* to discuss what we have called *expressive*. The characteristics of this kind of caring are a nonrational, subjective approach, interaction between teacher and student, circumstance bound decisions, and intuition/faith.

We suggest that the language of the expressive has often been seen as being in conflict and even in opposition to the technical. We propose that we have seen, and continue to see, the result of this oppositional view in the discourse about education among academics, practitioners, and the public. In examining examples of the everyday lives of practitioners and students of schooling, we are able to see how these two languages interconnect in the lives of those in schools. Whereas we in social science and academe insist upon separating and dichotomizing these notions, it is clear that, in the lives of those within schools, these distinctions are carefully interwoven and constructed.

It is in three aspects of schooling that we are able to see how the languages of the technical and expressive are intricately woven together. We have called these three aspects *intrasubjective*, *intersubjective*, and *organizational*.

The Warp: The Intrasubjective Meanings of Caring

The *warp* of a tapestry forms the foundation for the weaving. It is the group of lengthwise threads that actually provides strength for the fabric. The warp provides the underlying texture and color for the weaving. In the same way the warp functions in the weaving, the intrasubjective functions in the context of education. What we mean by the intrasubjective is the internal meaning system the individual brings to his or her role in the educational setting. These internal meaning systems are often unarticulated and unexamined. They are generally culturally derived.

The portrait that Kendrick, in her chapter, refers to as a genuine educator clearly emerges in the description of Annie Sullivan as "bold, largely self-taught, always ready to trust her own instincts, a risk-taker, but steadfast and determined at all times to will the child's best interests; humorous, self-deprecating and tough-minded; full of compassion." The degree to which the Annie Sullivan model of teacher is culturally derived becomes apparent as similar descriptions of teacher are repeated in other well-known literary pieces—a depiction of genuine or real teacher that, we assert, we all would find familiar.

Rogers's chapter, "Conceptions of Caring in a Fourth Grade Classroom," further develops the cultural models students and teachers have inherited regarding the role of the teacher. This work also demonstrates the degree to which judgments about good and bad teaching are influenced by these internal representations or meaning systems. The views of the children in Rogers's study were congruent with those of their teacher(s) with regard to their view of a caring teacher. Not unlike the image of the teacher personified by James Leeds in Kendrick's work, the caring teacher is described as "a person who is sensitive to the children's needs and able to understand things from their perspective; a just human being who seeks connection with his or her students; a person who is confident enough to let his or her students make mistakes and give them another chance. A caring teacher, finally, is somebody who is willing to take chances and design and implement an interesting curriculum while providing a safe and secure environment for learning."

The impact of internal meaning systems is clearly portrayed in McLaughlin's description of the experiences of three student teachers. In interviews with these student teachers he discovered different ways in which these women thought about caring for their students. He was then able, over the course of a semester, to observe how these personal representations of caring impacted their beginning work with high school students.

Eaker, in Chapter 8, provides an example of internal meaning systems from the perspective of women in higher education. She describes the women in her study in a position of reacting to the cultural model of the serious academic. These women heavily valued mentoring students and teaching over their research responsibilities. The attention and dedication they offered their own students had not been typical of their personal experiences in graduate school. They saw their choices to relate to students in this caring manner as contrary to the usual approach to university teaching.

The intrasubjective, as demonstrated through these examples, is essentially the culturally derived meaning systems that various players bring into the educational setting. Even though these meaning systems are often unexamined and unarticulated, they still profoundly impact the daily occurrence of schooling as individuals act out those meaning systems. As the warp provides the foundation or the background of the weaving, the intrasubjective provides the context in which caring in education can occur.

The Weft: The Intersubjective Negotiations of Caring

The warp alone, as we have described it here, is not sufficient to create a tapestry or to hold it together. With only the warp, the tapestry is void of any real life: It is, in fact, not a tapestry at all until the threads of the warp exist in relationship to the threads of the *weft*. Each thread in the weft crosses the threads in the warp. In the same way, individuals in their various roles in education act in relationship to others. In the context of these relationships, caring is either expressed or not expressed and experienced or not experienced. Noddings (1984) describes caring in relationships. We would take this a step further to include the negotiation of caring relationships that may include negotiation of meaning systems. Negotiation opens up the possibility of redefining *caring* in specific contexts. From this perspective, caring may look different in one school than another or may vary in classrooms within a school.

Rogers's chapter, as illustrative of the intersubjective, provides a clear picture of the fourth-grade classroom he studied. He describes a relationship in which the children feel cared for and in which the teacher feels she is caring. It is clear in this classroom that the teacher and students have worked out a common meaning system. Dempsey, in Chapter 5, also describes a give-and-take between teacher and students. He provides examples of teachers' descriptions of feedback from their students and how they use that feedback to confirm if what they are doing is working for the students. In this way a shared meaning system and a mutual understanding of caring can be negotiated. In Chapter 7, by Jaci Webb, two levels of the intersubjective are manifest. First, we see the internal negotiation of ethical researcher "images"; that is, the negotiation of the learned, "appropriate" researcher images with those images demanded by the situation of the research on caring. On the second level, as in the previous two chapters mentioned by Rogers and Dempsey, we see the continual negotiation of the relationship between teacher and researcher.

Essentially, the previous examples illustrate individuals negotiating relationships within educational settings. What becomes clear in all the examples is that these negotiated relationships depend upon, first, the *particular* people involved. In these relationships, teachers, students and/or researchers negotiated with one another. The second point that these examples show is that these negotiations are *complex*, *multidimensional*, and *happen over time*, unlike the sometimes static view one can get within certain ethnographic "snapshots" of classrooms and schools. If we begin to view these relationships (and others like them) collectively, it would be possible to see patterns of relating emerging in schools and other educational institutions. This perspective opens up the opportunity for creating consciously constructed organizational cultures of caring within educational settings.

Patterns of the Tapestry: Organizational Patterns of Caring

When we step back and look at a tapestry as a whole, the patterns become evident. The patterns created out of the various strands of the warp and weft make the tapestry as a whole cohesive and even logical in some senses. It is in this way that we can view educational organizations.

Educational organizations are comprised of a multitude of negotiated relationships. When patterns of negotiated relationships are discovered in educational settings, these patterns reveal the *particular culture* that holds the organization together. The consequences of these patterns become apparent and understandable, even if not always seemingly desired or agreed upon. We believe these patterns of negotiation are largely unconscious and unplanned. Thus, often the conflicts and upsets in organizations are a result of this unconscious process.

As described earlier, if one were to stand back and look at the entire tapestry we are calling *education*, certain patterns would be visible. The way an individual school operates could be described as having certain qualities, textures, and patterns that distinguish it from another school. Patterns could be seen from school district to school district and even from society to society. However, we assert that the tapestry of education has been largely accidental. It is rarely like the carefully planned tapestry of a master weaver.

In the following two examples, from the chapters by Danin and by Courtney and Noblit, we will contrast two organizational patterns of caring—one mandated and one consciously negotiated—to illustrate the hazards of an accidental process as well as the possibilities inherent within a conscious process of negotiation.

In the story told in Danin's chapter, "Contradictions and Conflicts in Caring," we see a school that *historically* was begun as a consciously created organizational culture set up to "get positive involvement for the teachers and students" and to "be a good place for kids." Seemingly, the project—that of caring for at-risk students—would be in line with the culture of the school as articulated. However, one can see in this chapter the consequences of assuming a consensus about the means and ends that should be used in such a project. Thus, several "elements" become apparent when looking at the results of a mandated project upon an historically consciously-negotiated culture.

First, we see in this story evidence of what Noddings (1984) describes as *aesthetic caring*, caring about ideas and things. As Danin suggests, such aesthetic caring exists when groups of people make decisions *about* other groups of people. What is not explicit in this description is the presumed legitimate authority of such groups to make decisions for the others. Certainly, we can imagine a scenario in which teachers could decide to institute a program for at-risk students, and, without the support of the administration, such a move would in actuality be a nondecision, at least officially. Thus, in the case here, it is key that the "aesthetic caring" to which Danin refers is seen as a decision made by those in authority (that is, the sponsors of the project, the superintendent and the principal) *for* the teachers and at-risk students. We suggest that such decisions may or may not be seen by those not consulted as caring of any sort, depending on the particularly intra- and intersubjective meanings of *caring* held by those "others."

The second element, a lack of consensus, falls logically into place from the first as seen in Danin's chapter. The teachers (and perhaps students although we do not know this), who were not consulted, do not agree that the project as defined is appropriately caring. This disagreement manifests itself early as a lack of consensus about goals, with the project goals being "global and idealistic" while the teachers goals were "daily and realistic." As the project continued, this lack of consensus about goals became concretely apparent: The valued goal for the administration was academic achievement, whereas the teachers saw the project, intended to improve achievement, as taking them away from the personal interaction they felt to be the first priority for any improvement with these students. Thus, academic achievement, for the teachers, was being subsumed under the appropriate goal of caring for their students.

The origination of the project from the outside sets the tone for the third element, appointed leadership. The members on the team to plan and implement this at-risk project were teachers appointed by the principal rather than self-appointed or elected. As Danin shows, the lack of involvement or ownership of the total school faculty resulted in further frustration that decisions were being made without democratic input. So the model of *aesthetic caring* out of which this project was conceived was replicated at the school level, where some teachers were making decisions for the rest. However, given the lack of official power of this group of teachers, these decisions resulted in discontent and strife among the teachers themselves in regard to the project and its accountability requirements. Rather than looking at the problems with the project as lying in the lack of caring and attention for the teachers and students in the decision-making stages, it can be argued on the surface, then, as is often done, that the teachers were the cause of the "failure" of the at-risk project.

The end result of this project, then, was the same as with much reform—resistance and minimal compliance by individual teachers and, thus, diffuse impact of change. What's more, as Danin demonstrates, the basic tenets of the original caring culture of the school were violated by this mandated project. The decision to implement this project did not involve open and equal dialogue which is foundational to any caring relationship and culture. As a result, there was no sharing and mutual negotiation of goals and actions in any sort of *genuine partnership*. Finally, and sadly, this historically created and shared culture was violated by the planning and implementation of the project: A loss of community resulted.

The second example, the chapter by Courtney and Noblit entitled "The Principal as Caregiver," shows how a project of a different sort was actually used as a means of consciously creating a negotiated caring culture. The principal in this case arrived in the midst of a confusing, turbulent period in the school's history. The major "job" he had, as he came to see it later, was to find a way to balance care and authority. As before, there are several elements of note in this consciously created culture of caring.

The two major elements used to create a new culture for the school was, first, a university–school partnership, and, more importantly, a democratic approach to leadership which included teachers, parents and the surrounding communities. Key to this effort was discovering what teachers considered being "taken care of." This discovery came while defining the oral history project, which was part of the university–school partnership. As might have been the case, this project, to reclaim the history of the school and community, could have been imposed by the principal without dialogue with teachers. Given dialogue, however, the principal realized that, while the project at the community and school level seemed beyond reproach, the basic question for the teachers was "what will it do for the children?" Thus, by paying attention to the teachers' concerns, minimal conflict resulted and the project was redefined to include the children in essential ways. This established the pattern of negotiated relationships between the teachers and the principal.

The oral history project also served as a relational link between the school and the surrounding communities, one of which had historically been closed out as the result of desegration. In order to reconstitute the history of the school, community members had to be interviewed. This process seemed to communicate to the two communities that the school "cared more." So, instead of becoming just one more thing to do as it might have been if mandated, the oral history project became a builder of school and community. As such, the school was increasingly moved toward and involved in creating an articulated culture of caring as the purpose of the school.

There were other elements of democratic leadership within the school culture which, on the surface, seem less original or unusual. For example, the principal took an approach to teacher evaluation that was more of a coaching relationship than traditional evaluation. As Courtney and Noblit describe, he worked with teachers in setting goals and professional development opportunities to accomplish their goals. Furthermore, he established connections between teachers, parents and the community by forming two advisory boards, one internal and one external. Finally, he demonstrated his care for (rather than authority over) the teachers by garnering new resources in conjunction with the university project, developing flexibility with present resources, and serving as a buffer for teachers by protecting them from unnecessary demands and increased workloads. As stated, some of these "management techniques" can certainly be seen in other literature on effective schools (see, for example, recent publications by Baptiste, Waxman, de Felix, & Anderson, 1990, and Holmes, Leithwood & Musella, 1989); however, what can be seen differently is that approaches to leadership and development that occur within a context of care have exponentially greater results than they might otherwise have. This, we argue, comes from the cohesive logic provided by a *consciously articulated* culture of care that establishes the environment for negotiated relationships to be ongoing and enabled, and more importantly, sets up the conditions under which they can.

In contrasting these two cases, we do not mean to suggest that there can be a template for creating the caring school. Rather we propose that an explicitly articulated and negotiated direction with caring as the context offers an educational culture consistent with the meaning systems of teachers. More importantly, it is consistent with the needs of children and families who are the major clients in education.

Implications and Conclusions

We consider the important clients of education to be children and their families, *and* we see the meaning systems of these clients to be congruent with those intrasubjective and intersubjective meaning systems of teachers. Given that, then the question asked by teachers, both implicitly and explicitly, in the chapters of this book should be the question by which all educational practice and policy implications should be drawn: The primary question by which we then must judge education would be "What will it do for kids?"

Certainly, we are neither naive nor ignorant of the political and practice implications such a question leaves us to confront. Within many of the chapters here, we see that the problem with absolute standards is that the clients with whom we should be primarily concerned have no voice in the process of negotiation or decision-making regarding those standards. As stated by Courtney and Noblit, the "bureaucracy of schooling does distort caring to meet its needs and structure. This critique needs to be elaborated and be used as a way to reconsider how schools should be organized if caring is to be the central logic." It is to this critique and possibility for educational organizations driven by caring that we now turn.

We began this chapter with reviewing what we termed the languages of the technical and the expressive. These languages become important in light of our question about children. Historically, we have made these two perspectives on education dichotomous and not without value, power, and gender implications. In general, until the advent of the academic discourse on caring, teachers have been the sole voice within the ranks of professional educators who have valued the expressive. Researchers and others within higher education have predominantly emphasized the technical in evaluating both teachers and schooling. As such, the discourse about teaching and education has not been between two equally valued and available perspectives on caring for children within schools. When those in bureaucratic authority value the technical most highly, then teachers are placed in a "forced choice" situation. They can implement the ideas of school reform promoted by the hierarchy and choose to subsume caring to the technical; alternatively, they can resist such reform ideas and be thought to be lacking in important ways (i.e., lacking in knowledge, expertise, training, intelligence, etc.). Thus, much of school reform and reform "failure" could be interpreted in light of this forced value choice. What has often been seen as teachers' resistance to authority may in fact be their commitment to caring for kids. Nonetheless, as long as we continue to hold the technical and expressive in opposition, and as long as those in legal authority continue to primarily emphasize standards, the message given is that the technical is what is valued. With that message, we are left in our current forced choice position.

We would like to offer the possibility that, rather than being a dichotomy, these two languages and their implications for educational practice are two sides of the same hand. We consider that it is indeed possible for both to occur simultaneously, although certainly not without profound and far-reaching consequences to current thought and structure. If we look slightly differently at Noddings's notions of aesthetic caring, we begin to get some clues.

Noddings (1984) considers aesthetic caring as being about ideas and things. She implicitly, it seems, devalues aesthetic caring, as if we had to make a choice between caring for people and caring about ideas and things. Ethically, we would hope that all those involved in education would value people more than ideas: Even so, one cannot, and would not wish to, strip education of ideas in the form of curricula, content, and the creation of knowledge. There are ideas to be dealt with and decisions to be made in regard to these educational components. We argue, however, that when these decision are made within an underlying and articulated culture of caring, the results of decisions, and probably many of the decisions themselves, would be very different than if made within an underlying culture of the technical. Decisions made within the frame of the expressive or the caring are consistent with the ethic of teachers, students, and presumably parents, as seen in this book. Decisions made within a culture stripped of the expressive are inconsistent and intolerable to many teachers, children, and parents at base. In saying this, we are not proposing to reverse the value choice and place caring at the top of a hierarchy to the exclusion of the technical. We are suggesting that, rather than an either-or choice, we can potentially derive an approach to education that would honor the value of both the expressive and the technical.

Assuming we can operate out of a position that holds both the technical and the expressive as valuable, what would schools and educational communities look like. The key to this orientation toward creating the educational tapestry would first and foremost be negotiated communication between people at all levels of education. Voices of practitioners, children, and families would be necessarily, and primarily, included in such negotatiated communication.

Alternative organizational and/or district structures could result. Within this context of negotiated communication, bureaucracy, by definition, would be incompatible as an organizational structure. While this would likely result in a nonhierarchical structure as well, we could possibly see the formation of a hierarchy for administrative purposes that nonetheless supports the negotiated culture of caring. For example, we could foresee as one possibility administrators whose negotiated positions would still be management. In this instance, however, management would likely take the form of managing resources and time to support the needs of children, teachers, and families.

It is not our purpose to write a prescription to continue the debate about the restructuring of schools and classrooms. Rather, we believe firmly that many of the current debates regarding education are ineffectual. These debates ignore the voices of the clients of schools, i.e., children and their families, and neglect the basic premise upon which teachers teach, i.e, that everything done in schools should do something worthwhile for kids.

Obviously what is worthwhile is culturally and contextually created and debated. We do not see it as possible or even desirable to definitively prescribe what is educationally worthwhile. We believe that, increasingly, such definition is what is being attempted implicitly and by exclusion. What we have to offer as a new possibility for education is the empowering that comes through negotiated communication. Negotiated communication is communication in which all voices are of equal value and in which caring can be seen as the context in which all educational decisions and relationships are ongoingly reconsidered.

Finally, we would like to offer a few reflections on the questions this expanded discourse and new possibility brings to mind for us. First, we would like to hear from others if our perspective, grounded in these chapters, resonates for others in the context of their work in education. In other words, when reading these concluding remarks, do these ideas seem to be something unconsciously "already known," yet when made conscious, do they have an effect that changes or alters the perspectives and work of others?

Second, we believe that there needs to be further consideration of the ideas about who participates in and how decisions are made within particular educational contexts. Therefore, additional grounded studies using the ideas and perspectives on caring and negotiated communication offered here are needed in existing educational settings, using methods determined to be appropriate within each particular context. Lastly, we would delight in seeing educators and communities consciously constructing and approaching the work of schooling from a culture of caring and negotiated communication. Within that conscious construction, we would hope that part of the negotiation would include research appropriate to systematically collecting information on how a conscious culture of caring is implemented and maintained. We would envision such research being in the form of action or collaborative research among the multiple parties to the project, but would certainly not want to predetermine what would constitute appropriate research within such projects. Certainly, this is not an exhaustive list but rather a series of concrete next steps toward investigating the usefulness and coherence of the ideas presented here.

With these ideas, we are back where we began, with the completion of the tapestry. A tapestry that is masterful must contain both the elements of technical and expressive excellence. There is no final "great work" for the master weaver but rather great works in process. May we go about the process of education with equal intentions of excellence and the commitment to always ask, "What will it do for the kids?"

REFERENCES

Baptiste, Jr., H. P., Waxman, H. C., de Felix, J. W., & Anderson, J. E. (Eds.). (1990). *Leadership, equity and school effectiveness.* Newbury Park, CA: Sage.

Goodman, J. (1988). Constructing a practical philosophy of teaching: A study of preservice teachers' professional perspectives. *Teaching and Teacher Education, 4* (2), 121–137.

Holmes, M., Leithwood, K. A., & Musella, D. F. (Eds.). (1989). *Educational policy for effective schools.* New York: Teacher's College Press.

Noddings, N. (1984). *Caring: A feminine approach to ethics and moral education.* Berkeley, CA: University of California Press.

Prillaman, A. R. (1988). *The acquisition of the role identity of teacher.* Unpublished dissertation, University of North Carolina, Chapel Hill.

Author Index

Subject Index